The Book of Modern Ceremony

The Book of Modern Ceremony

Practices to Mark Life's
Big and Small Moments

SHARI DUNBAR BOYER

Copyright © 2025 by Shari Dunbar Boyer
Photos copyright © 2025 by Lauren Purves

Hachette Book Group supports the right to free expression and the value of copyright. The purpose of copyright is to encourage writers and artists to produce the creative works that enrich our culture.

The scanning, uploading, and distribution of this book without permission is a theft of the author's intellectual property. If you would like permission to use material from the book (other than for review purposes), please contact permissions@hbgusa.com. Thank you for your support of the author's rights.

Workman
Workman Publishing
Hachette Book Group, Inc.
1290 Avenue of the Americas
New York, NY 10104
workman.com

Workman is an imprint of Workman Publishing, a division of Hachette Book Group, Inc. The Workman name and logo are registered trademarks of Hachette Book Group, Inc.

Design by Rae Ann Spitzenberger
Cover and interior photography by Lauren Purves
Photo styling by Alexandra Poer
Shutterstock: Dmitr1ch (linen texture); Chorna_black (frame); New Line (pattern); Vasya Kobelev (flourishes)

The publisher is not responsible for websites (or their content) that are not owned by the publisher.

The Hachette Speakers Bureau provides a wide range of authors for speaking events. To find out more, go to hachettespeakersbureau.com or email HachetteSpeakers@hbgusa.com.

Workman books may be purchased in bulk for business, educational, or promotional use. For information, please contact your local bookseller or the Hachette Book Group Special Markets Department at special.markets@hbgusa.com.

Library of Congress Cataloging-in-Publication Data is available.
ISBN 978-1-5235-2779-3

First Edition September 2025 APO

Printed in China on responsibly sourced paper.

10 9 8 7 6 5 4 3 2 1

For Christopher, Tristan, and Dylan:
my source of purpose and unconditional love

⇶

For Mother Earth:
my greatest teacher, guide, and inspiration

CONTENTS

An Invitation ix
What Is Ceremony? x
How to Plan and Hold a Ceremony 10

Circle Ceremony
37

Seasonal Ceremonies
43

Ceremonies for Life Events
77

Ceremonies for Personal Growth
149

Plan Your Own Ceremony 178
Resources 184
Acknowledgments 187
Index 191

An Invitation

I believe that all humans are yearning for meaning and connection in their lives. Modern society has left us exhausted, anxious, and separated from ourselves, each other, and Nature. Ceremony is a way to reconnect to something greater, a way to create meaning, and a way to create community. Each of us descends from a culture that used ceremony, no matter where our ancestors were from, and it is time for us to reclaim this heritage.

My greatest wish is that this book will provide inspiration for you. I invite you to read it in reverence as a ceremony itself. Let the book and its magic wash over you. Create a small ritual every time you pick it up. Light a candle, close your eyes, breathe deeply, and feel the living world all around you. Feel the collected wisdom this book represents, and let it make its way into your being. Note what catches your attention and what speaks to you. This is not random; it has meaning. Your soul is speaking to you through your senses. What you see and feel as you read has profound significance. Quiet your mind so you can listen to your heart. Each time you pick up the book, something new may speak to you. Honor this wisdom and your inner knowing.

> Ceremony ... is a process in which the human capacity for sacred feeling and reverence is given form and expression.
>
> —STEPHEN HARROD BUHNER

This book is for all of us. We are craving the meaning and connection that ceremony provides and have simply forgotten. Let the ideas and messages contained here guide you to remembering that you are connected—to other people, to Nature, and to the Divine.

WHAT IS CEREMONY?

Ceremony is one of the oldest "technologies" used by humans. As long as we have been living together, we have used ceremony to mark occasions, weave communities together, create meaning, facilitate transformation, and bring the Divine into our lives.

The word "ceremony" originates from the Latin term *caerimonia*, which means "a religious rite or worship." This term is deeply imbued with the notion of solemnity and reverence, highlighting the sacred and ritualistic aspects of ceremonies. Over time, the meaning of ceremony has expanded beyond just religious contexts. Now, ceremonies can refer to cultural and spiritual activities and rituals as well.

Every society on Earth has used, and still uses, ceremony in some form. Historically, ceremony was incorporated into many facets of life, including marking the change of seasons, divining the best planting times and locations, guiding loved ones to the spirit world during death, transitioning young people into adulthood, and harmonizing groups before making important decisions. In our modern world, most ceremonies are confined to either the religious realm or the Big Three—Birth, Marriage, and Death.

In ceremony, we leave the everyday world behind, journeying to a sacred space for a period of time. In this sacred space, we can connect to a collective consciousness, the wisdom of our ancestors and natural elements, and our own intuition. We each carry inside us the wisdom of all humanity, though we have trouble remembering this wisdom on a daily basis. By leaving our

daily worries behind and journeying outside of time and space, we can touch our inner wisdom, which creates healing, acceptance, and purpose in our lives.

A ceremony is a series of actions taken in a specific place, with an intention, by a group or an individual. The intention, the specific location that becomes sanctified through symbols, and the awareness and focus of the participants create the conditions for transformation or healing to occur. During ceremony, we enter an altered state in which we are more receptive to new meanings, patterns, and ideas.

> **Ceremonies are the way we remember to remember, and by remembering, we honor the gifts of the past and use them to construct our future.**
>
> —ROBIN WALL KIMMERER

The ceremonies in this book invite you to enter this altered state, one you may not be familiar with. That's okay. As you perform the ceremonies, try to remain open. You may experience new feelings, and you will begin to understand the language of symbols, the elements, and the heart, which are different from the language of words that we use every day. It may be uncomfortable at first, but trust that on some level, every ceremony you take part in with an open heart is creating meaning and change within you.

Additionally, though ceremony is performed in this earthly realm, healing or transformation can occur in other realms or levels of consciousness. Many symbols used in ceremony hold meaning across realms and can help carry messages across the boundaries between realms. You may experience wisdom or healing from your ancestors in the past or from forces unknown to you from the future. This wisdom may not be apparent to you during ceremony, and it requires a bit of openness and faith to receive, even when you cannot feel it or understand it in your conscious mind. This is the power of ceremony.

Often people ask what the difference between ceremony and ritual is. There are many definitions, but in this book, we will use "ceremony" to mean something that is performed for a specific purpose at a specific time and place, and though it may be repeated, it is never the same. It exists only once in time. Ritual is something that is performed regularly and frequently in a repeated pattern to bring awareness or mindfulness to the act. Both are important and bring meaning to our lives, but generally, ceremony is a more involved, thought-out, and elaborate act, whereas a ritual might be very small and repeated often. In addition, let's define the difference between "a ceremony" and

A note about cultural appropriation

Every traditional society used ceremony, which means *you* have a cultural legacy of ceremony in your lineage, whether your ancestors came from Europe, the Americas, Africa, the Caribbean, or anywhere else. That being said, there are some cultures that still actively practice ceremony and others that do not. The practices in this book are inspired by various cultures, and therefore, I ask that you acknowledge any cultural lineage that is referenced in the ceremonies. There is a very fine line between borrowing and stealing, and unfortunately, many ceremonies are often reproduced or disassembled by majority groups without respect to their cultural significance. It is natural to be inspired by cultures other than your own, but proper reverence and acknowledgment should always be given to the ideas and symbols you borrow. You can start by stating appreciation and acknowledgment for the culture from which the ceremony is inspired, similar to how many acknowledge prior inhabitants of the land that they are on. This is not enough, of course, to mitigate the harm of cultural injustices, but in this small way we recognize our inability to correct these injustices and proceed with humility. When appropriate, I have acknowledged the culture or lineage the ceremonies in this book are inspired by.

being "in ceremony." *A ceremony* is the occasion and physical act of performing the steps included in this book. Being *in ceremony* is more of a mindset where you are in a state outside of everyday time and space. Another way to think about it would be to compare it to going to *a church* versus being *in church*, which is more than just the physical structure.

The Purpose of Ceremony

The purpose of ceremony is to create meaning, transformation, or healing.

As our world has become more secular, technological, and individual, we have lost connection to rites, to the natural world, and to other people. This loss of connection has left us feeling alone and without purpose. Ceremony can help bring meaning back into our lives, particularly during transition, and can help connect us to others and the mystery of the Divine.

By focusing your energy, thoughts, spirit, and mind into performing the acts in this book, you will create meaning from something that may otherwise lay dormant. You will create a sense of control over transitions in your life, helping you take a more active role in changes both big and small.

Ceremonies can be performed alone, but they tend to be more powerful in groups, where you have the added benefit of synchronizing each member into a unified whole, a sum greater

---

The very act of assembling is an exceptionally powerful stimulant. Once the individuals are assembled, their proximity generates a kind of electricity that quickly transports them to an extraordinary degree of exaltation.

—ÉMILE DURKHEIM

than its parts. For each ceremony in this book, you will find a suggestion for performing the ceremony solo, in a small group, or in a larger group. You can determine the size of the group that feels right for you.

Taking part in group ceremonies is one of the most gratifying experiences we can have as humans. There is a reason that ceremony has lasted throughout the ages—it enriches our lives and creates a feeling of belonging. We seek this feeling at sporting events when we participate in the "wave" and at rock concerts when we sing along with the band, often coming away with a sense of extreme exaltation. Creating ceremony allows you to re-create and bring these sentiments into your everyday life.

> When we heal ourselves, we heal the world. For as the body is only as healthy as its individual cells, the world is only as healthy as its individual souls.
>
> —**MARK NEPO,** *The Book of Awakening*

In addition to creating meaning, marking an occasion, or facilitating transformation, some other reasons to hold a ceremony include:

- Creating shared purpose in a group
- Sealing intention
- Connecting with the Divine
- Reducing stress and worry
- Bringing awareness to an act, event, or feeling
- Purifying emotions or an environment
- Allowing the release of what is no longer serving
- Initiating healing
- Transmitting cultural values
- Moving from one phase in life to another

The ceremonies that follow will help you clarify and achieve your intentions. As you read, let the ceremonies wash over you, let them speak to you. Think of them as your partner or guide in going through the ups and downs of life. There is wisdom here, wisdom that you carry inside yourself and simply need to remember. Ceremony can be your bridge, so surrender to the mystery and let it guide you.

HOW TO PLAN AND HOLD A CEREMONY

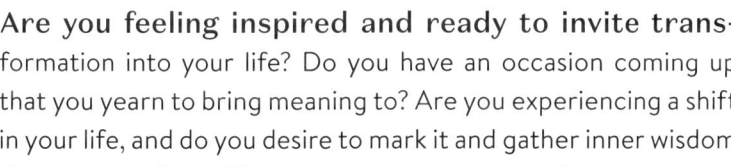

Are you feeling inspired and ready to invite transformation into your life? Do you have an occasion coming up that you yearn to bring meaning to? Are you experiencing a shift in your life, and do you desire to mark it and gather inner wisdom through the change? You are ready to plan your first ceremony!

Great! Now what?

How do you go about planning it to make sure you get the result you're hoping for?

The steps that follow are meant to guide you through a thoughtful process for creating a ceremony. Each ceremony in this book is presented as a recipe, with a list of suggested elements and step-by-step instructions. Please use them as templates or starting points and modify as feels best to you. The ceremonies are meant to inspire you to create something uniquely yours. I invite you to follow your gut. If something feels right to you, try it. Remember: All you truly need for ceremony is an open, loving intention and a symbolic act to represent the creation of meaning or transformation.

A Ceremony Planning Worksheet is included at the end of the book and can be found online at shariboyer.com.

Intention or Purpose

The most important step you can take to create the outcome you are seeking is to define the purpose of your ceremony. Be as clear and specific as possible. For example, instead of saying "to celebrate my birthday," you could say "to honor my ancestors and community and acknowledge the abundance in my life."

Here are some suggestions for setting a purpose or intention for your ceremony:

» **Be specific:** Being very clear and specific, even narrow, in defining your purpose does two things—it helps the participants understand what you are trying to achieve, and it helps you get clarity on why you are gathering and holding a ceremony.

» **Drill down:** Keep asking yourself why until you get to the *real* reason you are creating a ceremony. For example, you might want to host a baby shower for a friend with the purpose of "celebrating Mom and helping to prepare her for motherhood." Why? "She is going to be a first-time mom and needs some support." Why? "Motherhood is overwhelming and many who have done this can lend some advice." Why? "Mom-to-be actually has many resources around her who can lend wisdom, time, tips, emotional support, and gear." So the purpose becomes to "prepare Mom for the life-changing event of becoming a mother by calling in the wisdom and support of her community so she will feel safe and supported in her journey."

» **Think broadly:** While you are being very specific, don't forget to consider what your ceremony can contribute to the broader ecosystem or community. It's not all about us; it's about the world, our environment, and our communities—think about what your ceremony can do to make the world a better place. For example, consider the difference between creating a birthday celebration that acknowledges your community and your ancestors instead of just focusing on you. Doesn't it feel like it brings more light to the world?

» **Work backward:** Think of what you want to change or be different because of your ceremony. If you did not hold your ceremony, how would things be, and how does holding your ceremony change things for the better?

» **Let your purpose be your filter:** Once you have a clear purpose, it will help with all other decisions: who to invite, where to hold your ceremony, what elements to include, and who might play the different roles in the ceremony.

Guest List

Now that you have a defined purpose, deciding who to include becomes a little bit easier. It is always less complicated to invite more people, and leaving people off the list can be challenging. Our nature and our society encourage us to include everyone we can. We are taught, "The more, the merrier." But to be true to your purpose in your ceremony, you want to follow two guidelines:

1. Include *only* those who will help meet your purpose.

2. Exclude those who threaten your purpose (no matter how well you know them or how obligated you feel to include them).

Inviting the right guests and the correct number of participants is absolutely essential to fulfilling your purpose. In terms of size, again, refer to your purpose. Is this a house blessing? Then the house occupants are essential, and if neighborhood and community are important, inviting some neighbors may be important. Using our birthday example, since you are celebrating your community and your ancestors, including a more extensive group may allow you to connect with people representing many parts of your life, but inviting too many will feel inauthentic.

Location

Sometimes, the location will be obvious, like at a school for a graduation ceremony, while other locations will take a little bit more thought—or, more accurately, feeling. As you hold your intention in your mind, close your eyes and try to feel what would be a good location for your ceremony. Is there a place that has special meaning to you and is connected to your intention? If you are doing a house-releasing ceremony when you are leaving a home, perhaps you choose the room you spent the most time in, or the room that feels like the energetic center of the home. If you are doing a vow renewal, perhaps you choose the location where you first met or the location of your first date. For a birthday celebration, you could ask yourself, "What location represents my community or my connection to my ancestors?"

Remember to consider your group's practical needs: Will you need chairs? Is there a plan for rain or elements? Does your location accommodate gathering before and after the ceremony? Can you create a sacred ceremony circle inside the larger space? Is the space protected from interruption?

Any location *can* work, and you will make the space sacred with the preparation work you do. Do not fret over location; just give it some intentional thought and feeling.

Elements

Each of the ceremonies in this book suggests elements or ingredients you can include to create atmosphere and meaning. As you plan your ceremony, consider what elements you will include, using the suggestions as a guide. Change them to whatever speaks most to you, just like a chef would choose seasonal items and adapt a recipe to fit the needs of the occasion. The following are some common elements used in ceremonies.

≫ **Altar:** Creating an altar with items that are significant to you and your purpose is not required but can be a vital part of creating a sacred space for your ceremony. If you decide to create an altar, place it at the center of your ceremony circle or at the front where all can view it. You can use a special textile or stand to visually mark the space. Each participant can be invited to add a personal item of meaning to the altar. Please do not think of the altar in a strictly religious sense (unless you are religious) but rather as a focal point and space for collecting items of meaning.

≫ **Music:** Music or sound can be a crucial element for a ceremony because it can help participants leave the everyday world and enter into a meditative or trance state together. You can use prerecorded music, live percussion such as drums or rattling, or singing. There are suggested playlists in the Resources section (see page 184), and choosing your playlist can be one of the most fun parts of preparation. Delegating the responsibility for the playlist to someone in your life who is musically inclined can also be an excellent way to invite participation.

≫ **Blessing herbs or incense:** Sacred herbs—such as cedar, copal, frankincense, and sage—or incense can be burned to bring focus to the sacred space and help transport participants away from their daily lives. Smoke also carries the words and prayers of the group, creating a psychological, spiritual, and physical link to other realms. You can use these herbs in their dried form or use prepared incense.

≫ **Representations of the four directions:** The four directions—East, South, West, and North—also correspond to the four classical elements—air (East), fire (South), water (West), and earth (North). It is common to "invite" the directions and their corresponding elements to a ceremony because they guide us in our lives consciously and subconsciously. Feathers, bells, or incense can represent East/air and wisdom. A candle flame can represent South/fire and energy. A body of water or water in a cup can represent West/water and creativity. Soil or rocks can represent North/earth and groundedness.

≫ **Objects from nature:** Nature is a powerful force and should be present in every ceremony. Even if your ceremony is held indoors, you can intentionally include elements from Nature to bring the spirit of Nature into your circle. Some suggestions include flowers, rocks, crystals, leaves, and pieces of wood or branches. When collecting items from Nature to include in your ceremony, please practice *reciprocity*: always ask permission from the plant or Earth, wait for an energetic response, do not take more than is needed, and express gratitude for what you receive.

» **Food:** Traditional foods or food offerings can be included in the ceremony itself, either on the altar or during the blessing. Food as offering is an ancient practice, used by almost every society. Enjoying a meal together is a great way to relax and to integrate after a ceremony.

» **Poems/readings:** Consider whether any particular poems or quotes will help express your intention or bring your group into coherence. There are some suggestions in the Resources section (see page 184).

» **Pen and paper:** Many ceremonies use the practice of writing on a piece of paper and then burning or burying it to release an intention into the world. Writing down messages or images that come to you during ceremony is a great way to remember them after you have left the trance or meditative state.

» **Tea:** Teas or special drinks can feature prominently in certain ceremonies; for example, Japanese tea ceremonies are a revered tradition. Your own special blend of tea or herb can be used before, during, or after a ceremony to create a feeling or connection with elements of the body and with the plant world.

Invitations

The invitation is an opportunity to set the tone for the ceremony and to begin preparing and harmonizing the participants.

The invitation should include the intention, the location, why participants were chosen, a description of what the ceremony will entail, and any preparation required. The more information you give in advance, the better prepared and more present your participants will be during the ceremony. Sending a detailed description in advance also allows participants to ask questions before attending. You want to create excitement and energy and remove any fear or uncertainty. Be sure to include

any requests regarding technology, such as your expectations around whether phones and cameras can be present.

An invite might be a detailed email, a handwritten letter, or a phone call. Do not be shy about requiring a bit of preparation. It can be as simple as asking participants to think about something, such as "What does friendship mean to you?" More detailed preparation could include reflecting on life wisdom for a young person's rite of passage or finding a special gift for that person. Many ceremonies in this book invite participants to bring a meaningful personal item to place on the altar, promising they can take it back home at the end of the ceremony.

Roles

You will play a critical role as the organizer of the ceremony, and it can also be powerful to enlist participants to be responsible for certain aspects of the ceremony. This ensures active participation and takes some of the burden off you. As you set up your ceremony flow, think about who can fill each role and ask for their participation in advance so they are prepared. You don't necessarily need to "rehearse," but you could do a walk-through so everyone knows what to expect. The following are some roles you might consider enlisting for your ceremony:

» **Ceremony organizer:** The person or group who decides to hold a ceremony and will set the intention for the ceremony, which is the most critical step. The organizer will determine the invite list, send the invitations, and choose the location.

» **Celebrant (leader of the ceremony):** The person who leads the ceremony will play a significant role. This is usually the person who sets the intention and organizes the ceremony, but not always. The organizer could ask someone else to lead the ceremony, such as a friend, priest, rabbi, teacher, or someone particularly adept at holding people's attention.

» **Helping roles:** It is wonderful to invite others to participate in creating the ceremony. As the ceremony organizer, you may enlist the help of others to play roles such as creating the altar, calling in the directions, tending the fire, creating the playlist, reading something, or performing drumming or rattling. It can be nice to have each direction called in by a different person in the group.

Preparing Yourself to Perform Ceremony

Because many people are not in the habit of performing ceremonies regularly, you may feel shy or nervous about beginning. Even if you have performed many ceremonies, it is necessary to prepare yourself before each new event.

You do not need to be trained or ordained in any way to perform a ceremony. You have everything you need inside you to be an excellent leader. When you perform a ceremony, you will feel the flow of this ancient practice around you. You can tap into that flow and let it guide you.

Practice, practice, practice. The more you enact ceremonies, the more powerful you will become. Start with some of the solo ceremonies in the book and move on to small groups of people you trust. When you experience the power of connection and meaning-making that comes from your ceremony, you will be encouraged to keep going!

Prepare yourself to perform a ceremony by following these steps:

» An hour before you begin, sit quietly alone in your ceremony space and close your eyes. If you cannot physically be in your ceremony space, simply imagine it. Breathe deeply and ground yourself. "Grounding" means feeling connected to the energy and stability of the Earth. You can do this by sitting outside on the ground or just feeling the sense of support the Earth provides.

» Begin to think about opening up your body and senses. First, clear your mind of any thoughts. Imagine a cloudless blue sky and nothing else. Now, scan down through your body and unblock any negative energy or blockages. Imagine bright white light rays showering down over your head and flowing freely all

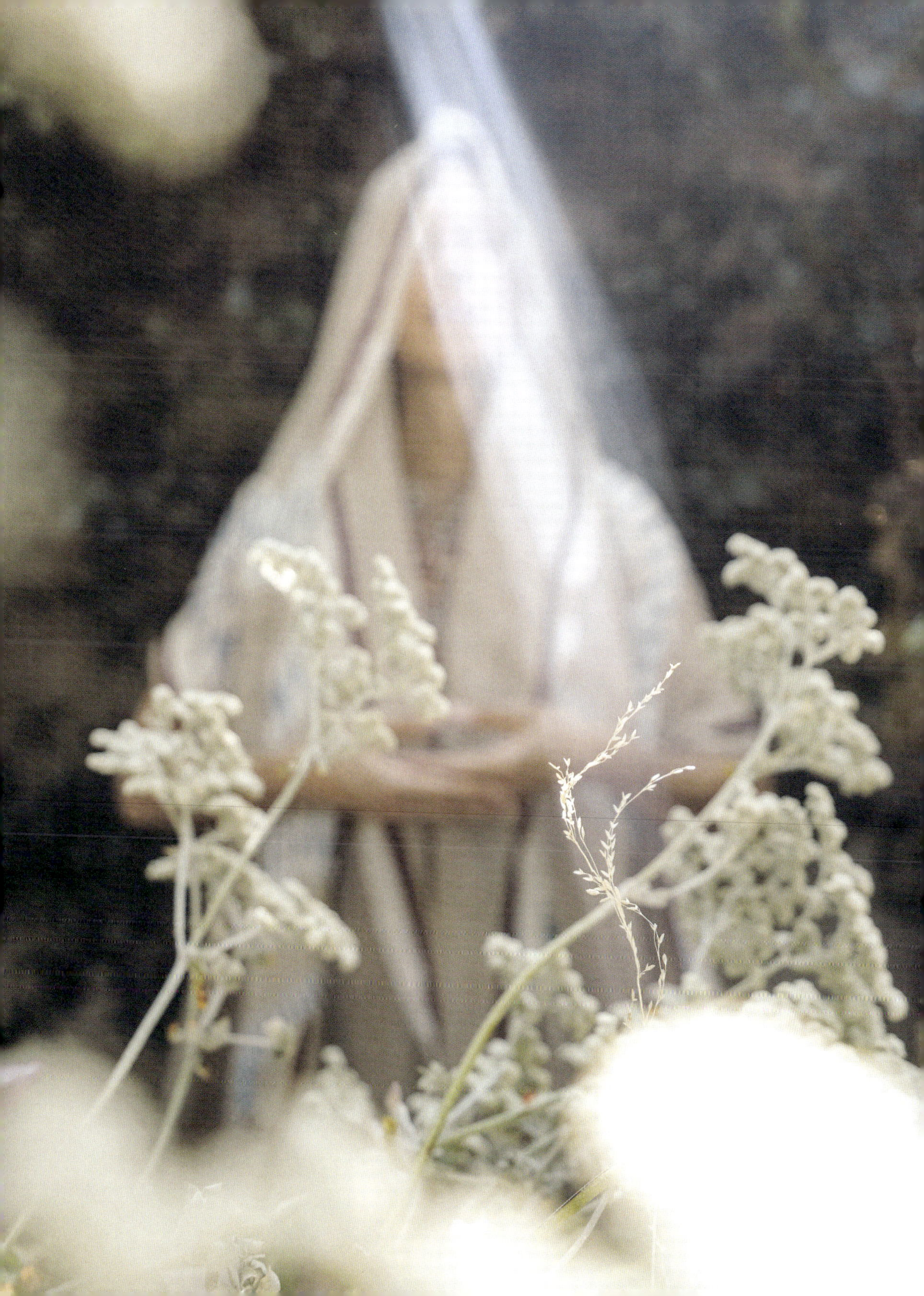

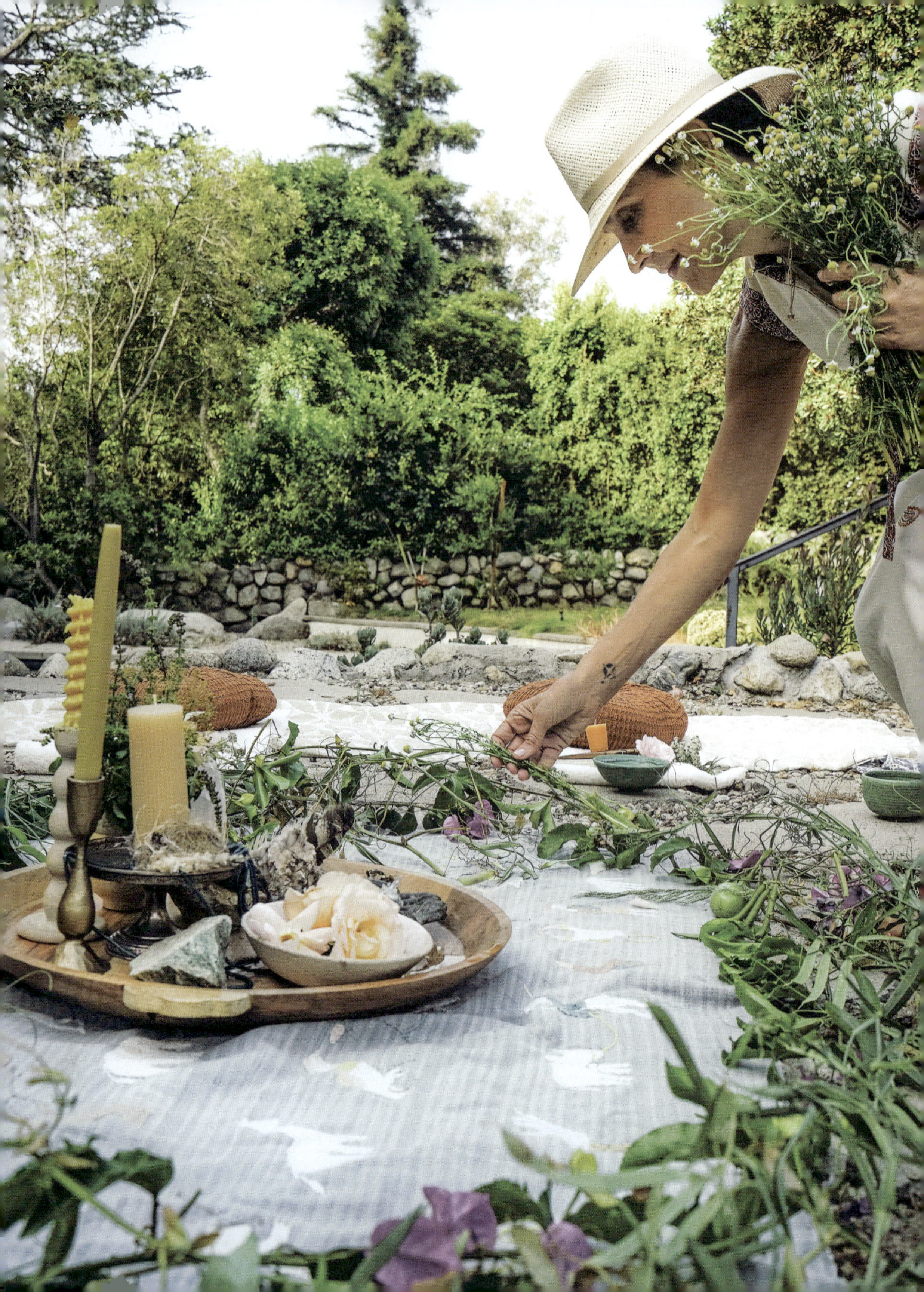

the way through your body, exiting through your feet. Do this until you feel clear and open.

⫸ With your body and your senses open and flowing, walk through the ceremony in your mind. Imagine the guests arriving, the steps you will take, how you will express the intention and perform the ceremonial act. Notice what flows freely and what feels stuck. Let the ceremony begin to take shape in your mind and body before it even begins. Say the words of the ceremony aloud until you become comfortable saying them naturally.

⫸ Open your eyes. You are prepared and ready. When the ceremony time arrives, remind yourself that you are clear and ready.

How to Hold Your Ceremony

Each of the ceremonies in this book has a suggested flow to follow from beginning to end. As you prepare, you can decide to follow the steps as given or change the flow to fit your purpose. Most ceremonies in this book include these steps:

⫸ **Set up your ceremonial space:** It is important to create a space that feels special and set apart from everyday life. Consider the act of setting up as the energetic and spiritual beginning of your ceremony. As you set up the space, keep your intention in mind and treat it with reverence and care. When setting up seating, a circle is highly recommended and allows all participants to have equal presence. Determine the best location for your altar, if you choose to have one, and lay it with care, leaving space for guests to contribute items to it. If possible, create a designated "entrance" to the ceremonial space through an arch, a path created with rocks or petals, a door, or a curtain. On the day of the ceremony, take extra care with the space by playing music and burning blessing herbs or incense to set the mood.

» **Gather the group:** All ceremonies start with gathering the group together. It can be helpful, but not necessary, to have a gathering space separate from the actual ceremony space. This way, you can gather, converse, leave belongings (especially phones) in a safe place, store food and drinks, and use the facilities before entering the ceremony space.

» **Enter the ceremony space:** When all have gathered, invite your group to enter the ceremony space you have set up. Ask your group to consider that they are entering sacred space. Invite participants to avoid talking while they enter. It can be wonderful to play mood-setting music. As they enter, the participants can place an item on the altar if they have brought one.

» **Welcome and harmonize the group:** When all participants are settled, begin the ceremony by welcoming them. State your purpose, explain the space you have created, and call attention to the altar and its meaning. Invite all participants to become fully present. Using a drum or rattle can help create a meditative state and synchronize your breathing. You can also choose to lead a guided meditation or play one that is prerecorded.

» **Invite the unseen:** If it feels right to you, invite the four directions and your ancestors, spirits, or guides to join the group. Choose the words and entities that resonate for you. Inviting the natural world and unseen entities into your circle is an important part of distinguishing this gathering from everyday life; however, this part of the ceremony can feel hokey to some, so adjust it as you feel comfortable. Each of the ceremonies in this book will have suggested language for this step, and you can modify as you see fit.

» **State your intention:** Clearly state the intention for your ceremony. Whether it is to celebrate a birthday or welcome a new season, it is necessary to remind everyone why they are gathered together.

≫ **Perform the ceremonial ritual:** Conduct the action or ritual that symbolizes the intention of your ceremony. Each ceremony in this book will have its own unique action or set of actions to perform. This step is the main part of your ceremony and will involve all participants.

≫ **Gather wisdom:** Once you have completed the ceremonial ritual, you will want to create space to gather the messages that have come through from your subconscious, your heart, or from ancestors or guides during the ceremony. Participants should allow these messages or pieces of wisdom to wash over them, sinking in. Allow time for this—it may take several minutes. Don't rush it.

≫ **Share:** To capture the messages or lessons of the ceremony, you can invite a few members of the group to share their experiences. What is different now that the ceremony has been performed? Are there any changes in feeling or personal transformations? Alternatively, you can invite the group to capture their insights by writing in a journal. Don't skip this step, as sharing the lessons as a group or in writing helps to solidify the wisdom in the minds and hearts of the participants and in the world. Coming out of ceremony is often like waking from a dream, and it can be hard to remember your thoughts and feelings later when back in the "real world."

≫ **Close the space:** It is essential to officially close your circle and release the elements, spirits, and guides who have joined you. Thank them for their presence and wisdom and let them know they are free to depart. Do this to the degree that feels

That, I think, is the power of ceremony: it marries the mundane to the sacred. The water turns to wine, the coffee to a prayer.

—ROBIN WALL KIMMERER

right for you. Before releasing your group, restate your intention in an affirmative statement as if it is now so. For example, instead of saying, "Thank you for celebrating my birthday," you can say, "Each of you and my ancestors are a vibrant part of my life and bring me abundance each day. Thank you for sharing this with me."

» **Celebrate:** Enjoy a meal or celebration together where you can share stories of the experience or just bask in the afterglow of the collective effervescence created during the ceremony. This will feel different than a typical gathering, and your group will likely feel enormously connected. Incredible bonds and sharing can be experienced during this post-ceremonial glow.

Post-Ceremony Follow-Up

The sharing you do at the end of the ceremony is extremely powerful; you can also consider whether additional follow-up will be helpful. This could be as simple as sending around photos or notes from the ceremony so that the wisdom continues to be present for participants. Perhaps you want to plan a monthly video call or get-together with participants to check in on how their intentions or projects are going. Thinking about this in advance and letting participants know will help set you up for success.

After the Ceremony

When you complete a ceremony, especially one that may be heavy or intense, it is important to clear the energy from your body. You can do this by washing your hands, taking a few deep cleansing breaths, shaking your body, and saying, "I release the energy of the ceremony." Repeat these actions until you feel clear.

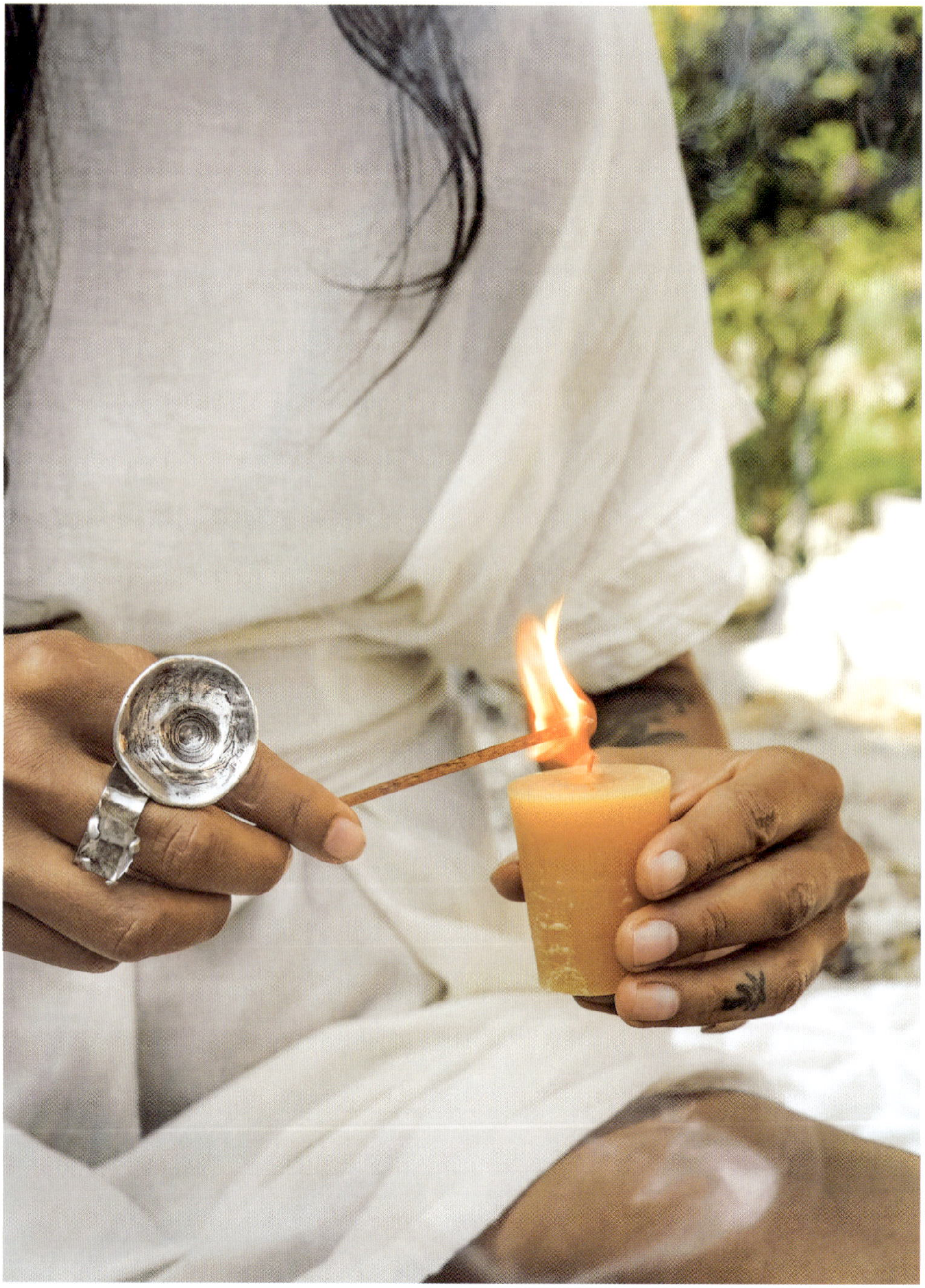

Common Symbols for Ceremony

The beautiful thing about ceremony is that it takes place in our real world but can create ripples in all realms or levels of consciousness. One way that we can communicate in other realms is through symbols. All of the ceremonies in this book will suggest the use of some symbols or tools. Particular objects in the list below are associated with a specific meaning, and of course, you can always use a symbol that has a special meaning for you. The following is a list of some common symbols or tools that can be used in ceremony, and their meanings.

- **Candle:** South, illumination, carrying messages through the air, fire
- **Feather:** East, air, wisdom
- **Bread:** nourishment
- **Branch of tree:** home and security
- **Water:** West, cleansing, purification, creativity
- **Fire:** South, transmuting or releasing
- **Cup or chalice:** unity, nourishment
- **Incense:** consecrating space, carrying messages with the smoke
- **Yarn or string:** tied for binding things together, cut for releasing something
- **Soil:** North, earth, fertility, growth, potential
- **Arch or doorway:** entering sacred space, moving from one phase to another

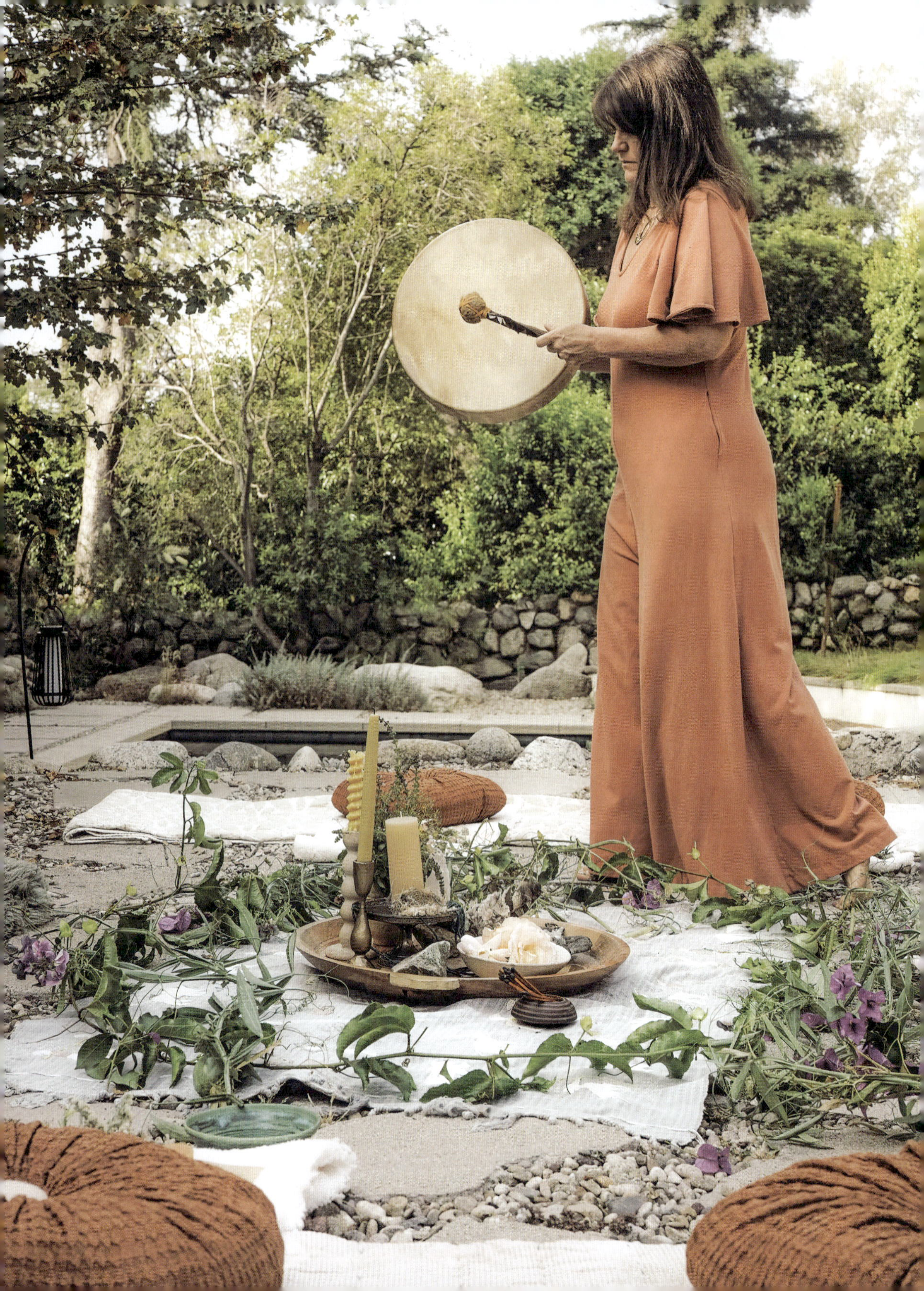

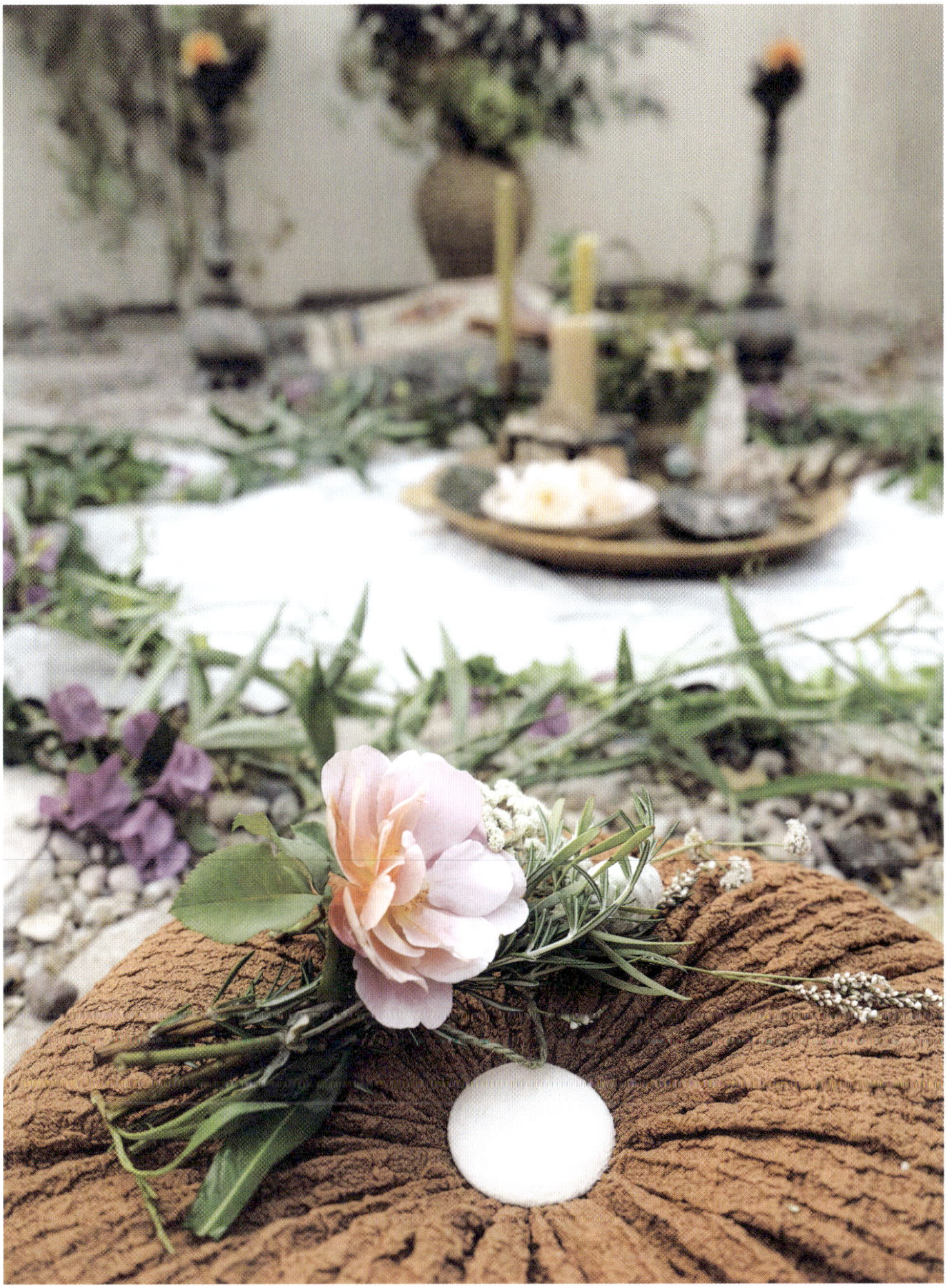

CIRCLE CEREMONY

To create
and nurture
community

The most elemental and powerful ceremony of all is also the simplest: the circle.

The circle ceremony involves nothing more elaborate than a group of people sitting together in a circle and sharing. Though the physical elements of a circle are elegantly simple, the spiritual alchemy that occurs is nothing short of transformative. This is not a space for advice or problem-solving, but for deep listening and radical acceptance. As we attune to the rhythms of the circle, our inner wisdom awakens. Wounds begin to heal, burdens lighten, and our most authentic selves emerge—not because someone has tried to fix us, but because we have created the conditions for our own innate healer to shine through.

Sitting in a circle with others is a profoundly human experience that fulfills our need to belong. When we gather in a circle to share and bear witness to each other, we embody the spirit of community—each person an important piece of the whole. Many ceremonies suggest forming a circle to perform a ritual act, but the circle itself is one of the most meaningful ceremonial acts.

In a circle ceremony, participants follow a simple set of agreements that help to foster open, honest, and meaningful communication. These agreements are useful for every ceremony in this book where participants share with each other, and it may be helpful to review them with your participants prior to beginning.

Circle Agreements

SPEAK FROM THE HEART
Participants are encouraged to speak sincerely, authentically, and spontaneously. This means you are not meant to decide in advance what to say but rather to see what arises when it is your turn to speak. This creates an atmosphere of trust and vulnerability and ensures that each circle is unique. Each share should also be *brief but deep*, respecting other members' time and keeping the energy focused.

LISTEN FROM THE HEART
As each circle participant shares, the others should aim to be fully present and attentive without judgment or response. It is also paramount that what is shared in a circle stays in that circle—shares are confidential, and usually it is agreed that participants do not discuss circle shares once the circle is ended.

ONLY THE SPEAKER SPEAKS
In a circle a talking piece is often used, and only the person holding the piece speaks. The talking piece can be anything: a stick, a rock, a crystal, a piece of yarn—the object does not matter, but only the person holding the piece can speak. When they are complete with their share, they can pass the piece to the next speaker, indicating their turn has finished.

Some circles have no topic or prompt, but you certainly could offer a prompt to the group if you like, such as "How are you right now?" or "I feel safe when . . ." or "What does acceptance feel like to you?"

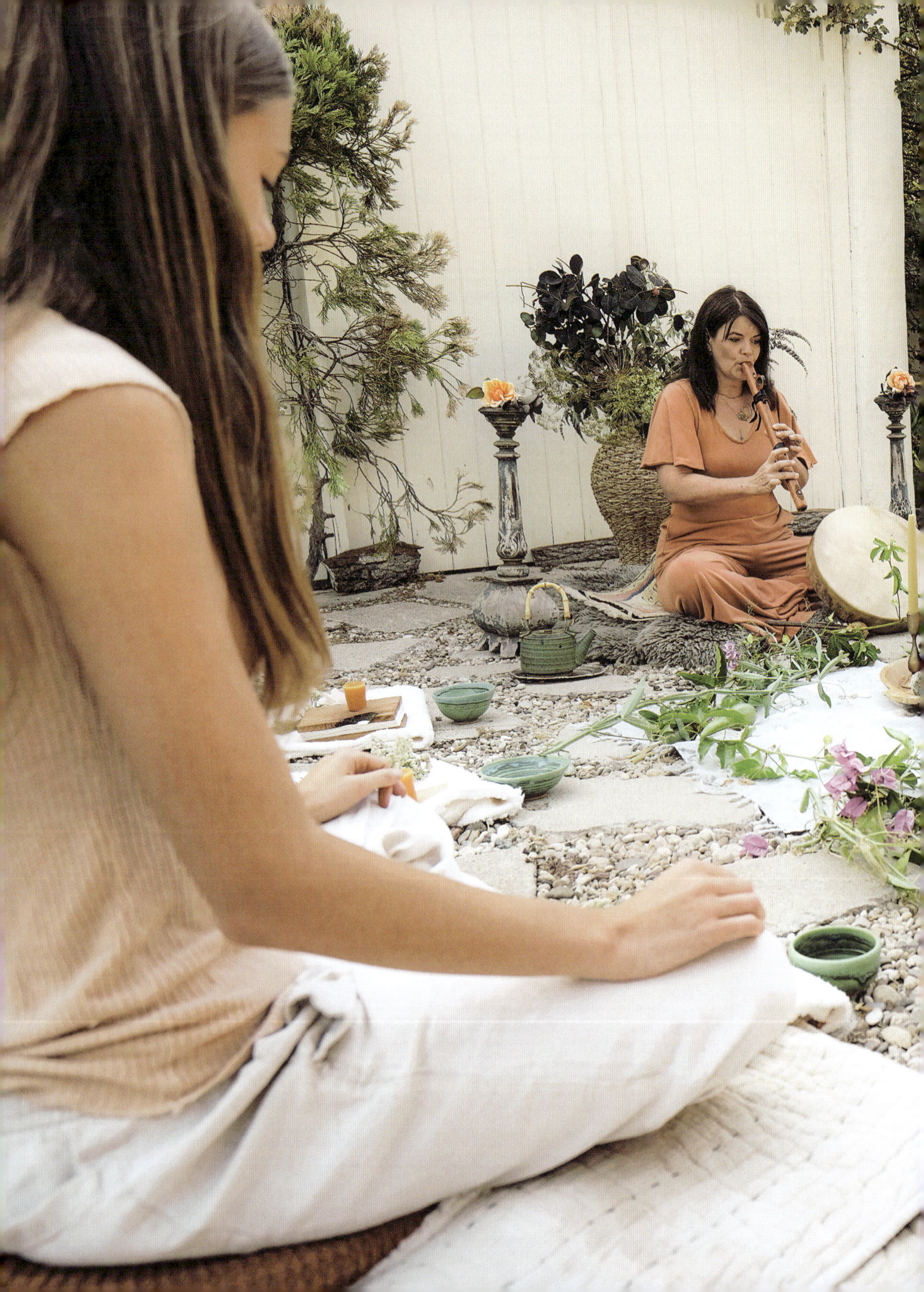

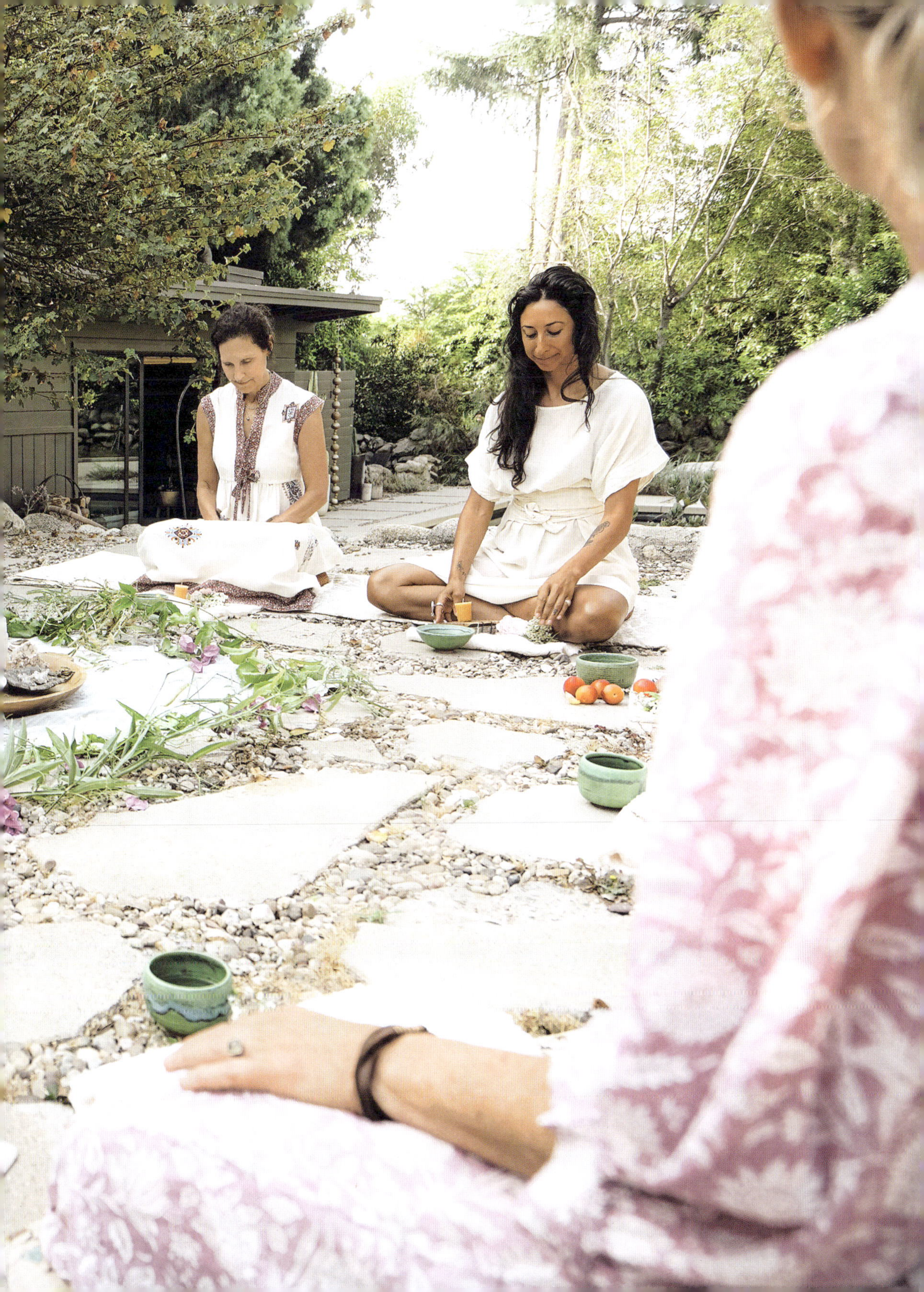

SEASONAL CEREMONIES

For harmony
and connection
with Nature

The ceremonies in this chapter will help you connect to the natural world and tune in to the cycles of Earth. Ancient societies planned their lives around moon cycles and the seasons. Our modern calendars are based on these cycles, yet many of us have lost touch with why we celebrate at certain times of the year. For example, many cultures celebrate Easter, which commemorates the resurrection of Christ, in early spring, just as the Earth begins renewing itself. Flowers and trees start blooming and many animals are born during this time, creating an emergent energy that pairs perfectly with this holy holiday.

Learning to pay attention to the cycles of the moon and seasons can show us how to live in harmony with the Earth, resting when she rests and being productive when she is productive. We can also infuse our traditional holidays with more purpose by creating ceremonies that connect us to each other and to the deeper meaning of the holiday, remembering with our inner selves why these holidays were created in the first place.

Moving through the year and honoring the Earth and her cycles in each phase can bring an entirely new meaning to your life and connect you much more deeply with Nature, something many of us are desperately missing in our lives. Start small. These seasonal ceremonies can be performed alone or with a small group, and they are very simple—just a pause in your life to reconnect to Nature and recognize your place within her great web.

CEREMONIES FOR

New Moon
48

Full Moon
49

Vernal Equinox
53

Summer Solstice
56

Autumnal Equinox
60

Samhain
63

Thanksgiving
66

Winter Solstice
70

New Year
73

SEASONAL

Moon Ceremonies

The moon plays an essential role in our physical world, governing the tides, which correspond to our internal emotional and spiritual world. The moon is sometimes referred to as "grandmother," for she holds wisdom and quiet strength. She follows a cycle where she grows and recedes each and every month while the sun shines on in its consistency. By reflecting on the moon's growth-recede-regrowth cycle each month, we can apply it to projects, emotions, relationships, and other parts of ourselves.

The new moon, or dark moon, is associated with birth and rebirth and is, therefore, a time for launching and allowing new beginnings to emerge. This is a wonderful time to state your intentions for your own growth, for a new project, or for a renewal in a relationship.

A full moon allows you to see things clearly. It is a great time to assess parts of your life honestly and to follow your intuition, which can be at its sharpest during a full moon. Consider releasing a feeling, project, or relationship you have seen to fruition during this time.

Moon ceremonies can be celebrated alone or in groups. The ceremonies here are designed for one person, but you can adapt them for multiple people. Since we have a new moon and a full moon each month, you have the freedom to celebrate them monthly or only when you feel called to mark the occasion.

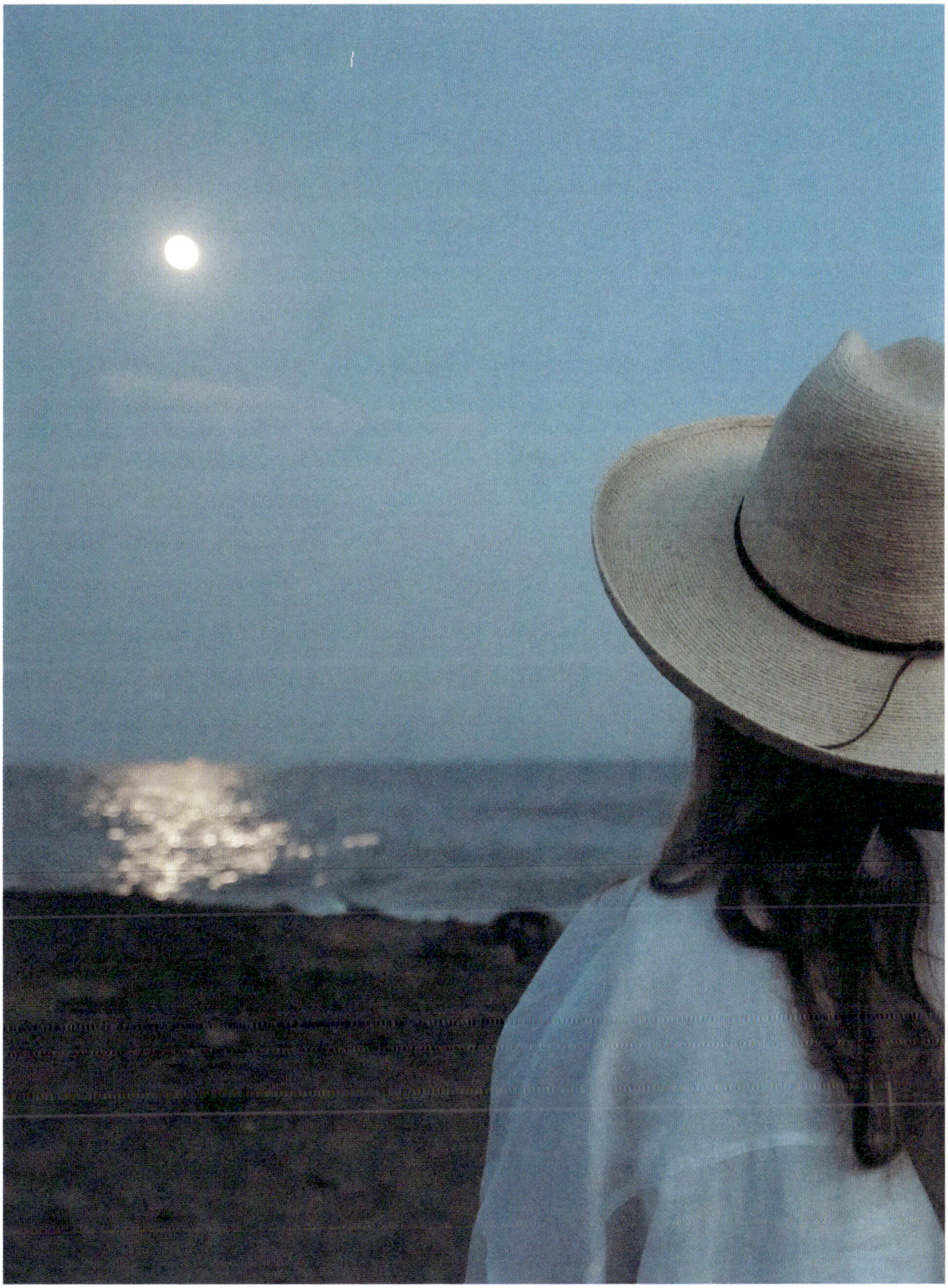

SEASONAL

≈ NEW MOON ≈

INTENTION

Launch a new mindset, project, or relationship or declare a new guiding thought.

SOLO CEREMONY

TIME NEEDED

15–30 minutes

ELEMENTS

Candle

A body or decorative container of water

Items that inspire or correspond to the season, such as leaves, rocks, crystals, photos, or jewelry

Journal or paper/pen

STEPS

» On the evening of a new moon, find a place to sit outside or near a window with a view of the sky. Create a small altar with your candle, water, and your inspirational or seasonal items.

» Light the candle and allow the glow of the flame to flicker over you. Leave all other lights off.

» Breathe deeply, connecting with the energy of the dark, expansive sky. As you exhale, release anything that is not serving you. You can say aloud, "I release _____ , which is no longer serving me."

» Ask yourself what is rising in you, wanting to be birthed into the world. Maybe it is a project, a trip, a relationship, or simply a new way of approaching your days. Sit quietly and listen for the answer with your whole body.

» Once you have clarity on what you would like to bring into the world, ask for the support to make it happen. What words of encouragement can you summon, what skills can you draw on, and who can help you? Open yourself to receive these messages. Feel the wisdom of the new moon enter your body.

» Write down your intention and the messages you receive in your journal. Keep this close over the next few weeks and know that it carries energy.

» Thank the moon for her wisdom and for supporting you as she begins her monthly growth cycle. Blow out your candle.

FULL MOON

STEPS

≫ Find a place to sit outside under the full moon. If you can't be outside, then sit near a window with a view of the sky.

≫ Light your candle. Harmonize your earthly body with the moon above by breathing in the energy of the full moon and feeling her light caressing your body. Imagine her love and wisdom washing over you.

≫ Ask a question that you are seeking an answer to. You could ask, "What is the best decision to make?" or "What skills or resources have I forgotten about?" or "What will serve my higher self at this time?" Breathe quietly, and let the answers come to you. Do not think too much; just breathe and let words, messages, or images appear. Feel the radiance of the full moon illuminating your inner wisdom. Let the light settle on your third eye, the seat of intuition, located on your forehead between your eyes. Feel the light of the moon represented in the candle in front of you.

≫ Accept the messages or affirmations you receive and write them in your journal.

≫ Thank the moon and the cosmos for the divine wisdom and illumination. Ask them to work with you as you manifest your dreams and intentions.

≫ Blow out the candle as you acknowledge the moon's radiance and wisdom one last time.

SEASONAL

INTENTION
Allow the full moon energy to illuminate your life and give you the vision to see things as they truly are.

SOLO CEREMONY

TIME NEEDED
15–30 minutes

ELEMENTS
Candle

Journal or paper/pen

SEASONAL

The Wheel of the Year and Marking Seasonal Change

The Wheel of the Year is a calendar that corresponds to Nature and the seasons. This modern calendar has roots in Celtic, Norse, and Germanic traditions and can be an excellent way to think about the year and the seasons of our lives. The Wheel of the Year has eight key points or festivals, including the solstices, equinoxes, and the midpoints between them (dates noted for the Northern Hemisphere).

- **Imbolc** (February 1)
- **Vernal Equinox** (March 20–23)
- **Beltane** (May 1)
- **Summer Solstice** (June 20–23)
- **Lughnasadh** (August 1)
- **Autumnal Equinox** (September 20–23)
- **Samhain** (October 31–November 1)
- **Winter Solstice** (December 20–23)

Observing these Nature-based festivals will allow you to sync to the Earth's natural cycles and bring yourself in harmony with Nature. For example, the Autumnal Equinox, the time of the traditional harvest, can serve as an annual cue to "harvest" your thoughts and feelings about the year to date.

Whether you plan a big celebration for these festivals or simply stay aware of the seasonal changes, bringing yourself and your life more in tune with the cycles of the Earth can benefit your health and well-being. For example, when we attune to the rest cycle that winter brings, we prepare ourselves for the blossoming energy of spring and gather strength for the production and growth cycle of summer.

The following ceremonies are used to mark the seasons not by the Western religious calendar but by tuning in to the energy of the Earth and the cycles of Nature.

SEASONAL

Wheel of the Year

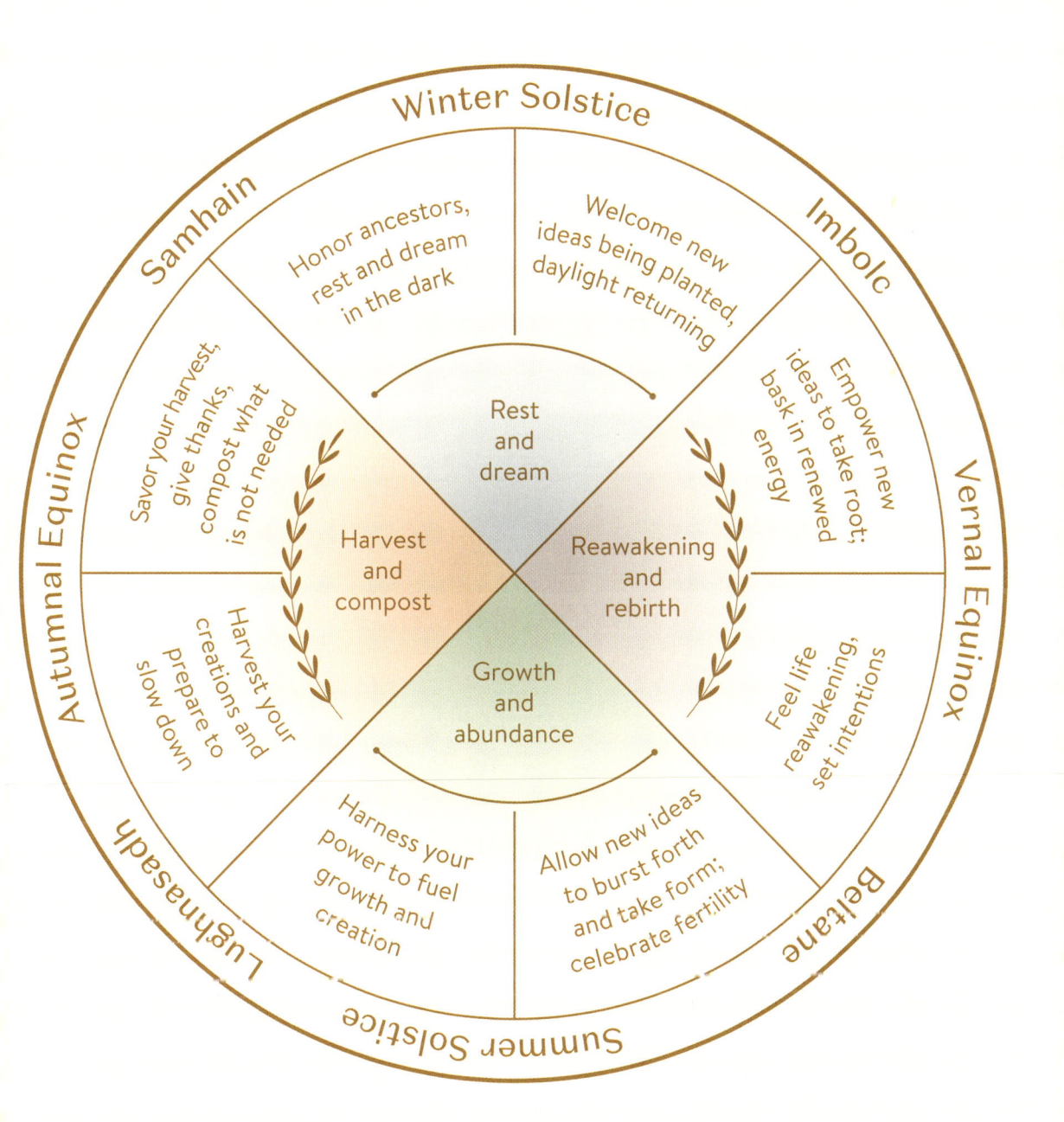

Winter Solstice — Honor ancestors, rest and dream in the dark

Imbolc — Welcome new ideas being planted, daylight returning

Vernal Equinox — Empower new ideas to take root; bask in renewed energy

Beltane — Feel life reawakening, set intentions

Summer Solstice — Allow new ideas to burst forth and take form; celebrate fertility

Lughnasadh — Harness your power to fuel growth and creation

Autumnal Equinox — Harvest your creations and prepare to slow down

Samhain — Savor your harvest, give thanks, compost what is not needed

Inner quadrants:
- Rest and dream
- Reawakening and rebirth
- Growth and abundance
- Harvest and compost

51

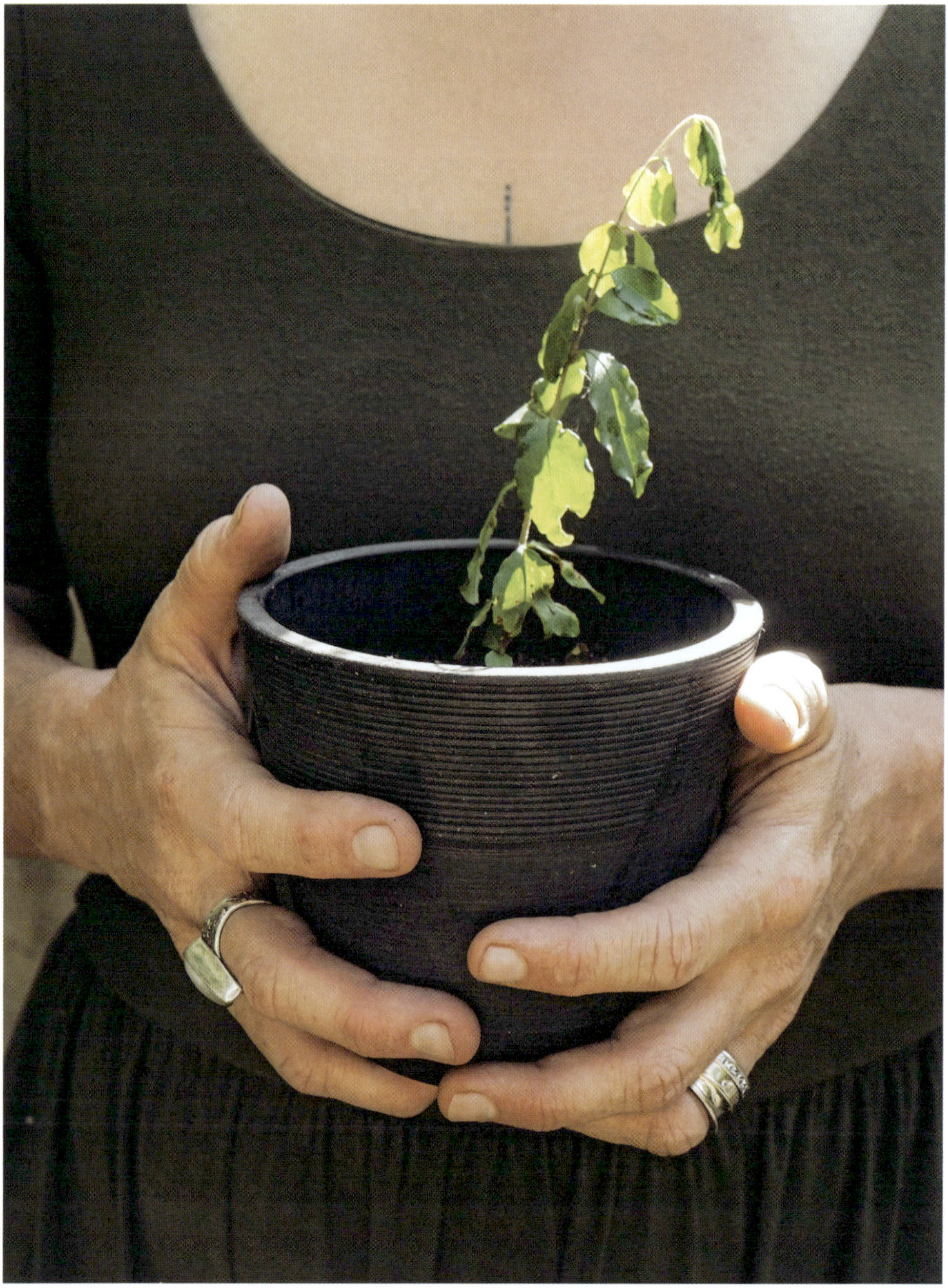

Vernal Equinox

The Vernal Equinox is one of only two days in the year where the light and dark are in equal balance, the other being the Autumnal Equinox. The Vernal Equinox signals the beginning of spring, the return of the sun, and, with it, longer, warmer days. This is the time of planting seeds and the celebration of making it through another winter.

This is a simple celebration to mark the start of spring, the quickening energy after the rest of winter, and the return of light. If you traditionally celebrate Easter or Passover, you can incorporate elements of this seasonal ceremony into your religious tradition.

STEPS

» Create a beautiful seasonal invitation for your group, asking them to join you in welcoming the new season. Invite each participant to bring a seedling or seeds that will represent an intention they wish to set for the new season.

» If it is warm enough, set up a ceremonial spot outdoors. If it is still cold where you are, you can set up near an outdoor firepit or inside by a window with a candle or fireplace. Create an altar with items that represent new beginnings, growth, and spring.

» Invite the group to enter the ceremonial space in silence, bringing with them their plant or seeds and any items they wish to place on the altar.

(continues)

SEASONAL

INTENTION
Welcome the spring with its energy of new beginnings and set a guiding thought for the productive growth seasons of spring and summer.

GROUP CEREMONY

TIME NEEDED
1 hour

ELEMENTS
Candle or fire source

Items that represent spring, such as flowers, eggs, or pastel ribbons

Seedling plants or seeds, soil, and pots

Herbal tea of mint, lemon balm, or an energizing herb

Biodegradable paper

Journal or paper/pen

SEASONAL

» Ground the group by pouring each participant a cup of herbal tea. Invite them to bring their mugs to their faces and let the aroma waft over them. Ask them to breathe in deeply, take a sip, and imagine the herb entering their bodies, warming and strengthening them from the inside. Invite the group to see if they can feel where the tea flows in their bodies and notice what sensations they feel.

» When all are energized by the tea, invite them to turn their attention to their seeds or seedling plant. Ask them to place their hands above the plant or seeds and offer to share their warmth and vitality with the plant. If you are working with seeds, invite each guest to ceremonially fill their pot with soil and plant their seeds in the pot. Invite each person to whisper a wish or desire for something they would like to grow in their life this year into the plant. Some examples are "I'd like to grow a deeper relationship with my sister" or "I'd like to become a better cook this year."

» Invite each participant to write their wish or desire on a small piece of biodegradable paper. If the ground is not frozen, you can plant the seeds or seedlings in the ground, along with the paper holding the wish. If the ground is still frozen, keep the seeds or seedlings in pots until they can be planted in the ground. Invite the group to feel the energy of new life that will begin to take root.

» Invite all to close their eyes and see if they can feel the quickening energy of spring in their bodies. Ask them to focus on the Earth, listening for or sensing signs of new life. Are there any birds singing? Invite all to open their eyes—are any shoots of new plants visible? Notice the Earth and her early stirrings as she wakes from the slumber of winter. Ask each participant, "What do you feel awakening in your body and life?" Invite each to write this down in their journal, even

SEASONAL

if it doesn't have much shape yet; they should just write down what comes to them. Invite the group to check back on these wishes when the sun is high in summer.

≫ Blow out your candle or let your fire burn down. Invite the group to remember that they can connect to the small fire inside them whenever they want to and know that the heat of summer is coming.

≫ You can invite members of the group to share their intentions or what they felt stirring in them, as speaking wishes out loud helps give them power.

SEASONAL

Summer Solstice

INTENTION

Celebrate the bounty and growth of summer and hold the feeling of abundance inside so that you can access it during the quiet of winter.

GROUP CEREMONY

TIME NEEDED

1 hour–whole afternoon

ELEMENTS

Table or picnic area

Items that symbolize the bounty of summer, such as fresh fruit, homemade jam, a favorite dish, flowers, poetry, and art

Extra place setting

Summer! It's the season of long days, growth, and high energy. Summer corresponds to high noon and to Mother Nature's busy phase. The Summer Solstice is the longest day of the year and the shortest night, a good time to celebrate light and abundance. This ceremony is a wonderful way to share a meal with loved ones, showering abundance and joy on all participants.

STEPS

» Create a beautiful invitation to request your loved ones to celebrate the solstice with you. Be sure to include your intention on the invitation and ask guests to bring something that symbolizes abundance in their lives—like fruit growing in their yard, a favorite dish, homemade jam, or art or poetry they created.

» Set a table outside and leave room for guests to place their offerings. This is a time for exuberance and excess! Don't hold back. Pile the table high with ripe fruits, vegetables, flowers, and offerings from Nature. If you'd like, set an extra place at the table for ancestors and place small amounts of each food on the plate for your ancestors to receive. In this ceremony the table itself is the altar, with each offering symbolizing abundance.

» When your guests have arrived, gather around the table and hold hands. Invite the energy of summer, associated with fire, heat, production, and abundance, to join you at your table. Go around the group and have each person state one

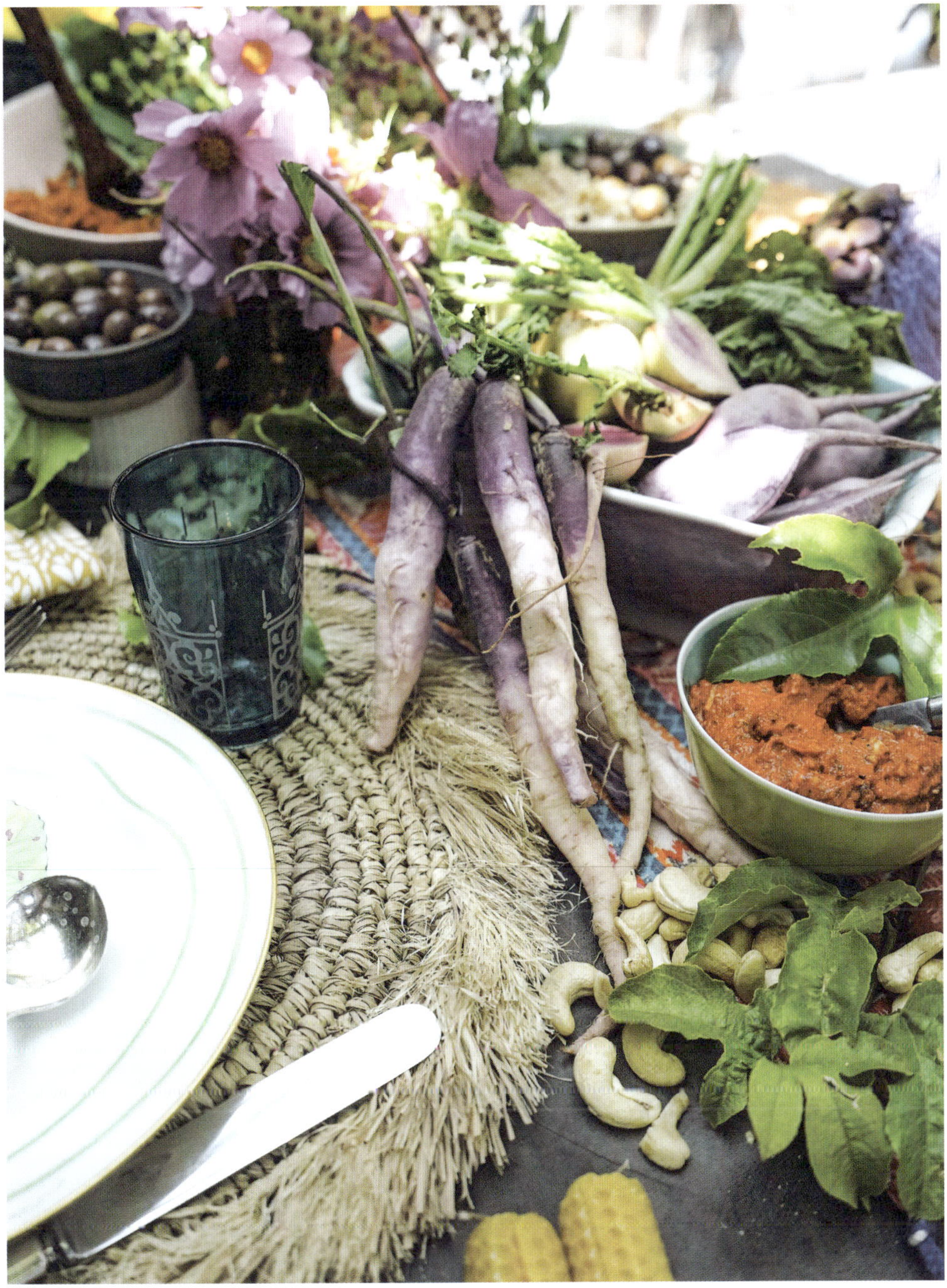

A CEREMONY FOR

SUMMER SOLSTICE

LET'S CELEBRATE THE LIGHT

SATURDAY, JUNE 21
7PM

Join us for a ceremony to celebrate the abundance
of Summer on the longest day of the year.
Bring an item to share:
Fruit from your yard
Homemade jam
A favorite dish
Artwork, poetry, or music
An item for the Summer altar

SEASONAL

word or thought that is coming to them as they stand in the middle of the year on the longest day. It can be a wish, a desire, or just a feeling. When all have stated their word or thought, thank Mother Earth for the great abundance she has provided and acknowledge all the hands that brought the bounty to your table.

≫ Sit and eat together. Give thanks for each bite, and marvel at the abundance around you.

≫ When you have finished your meal, it can be wonderful to extend the ceremony around a fire, symbolizing the heat of summer. As you are gathered, speak of all the abundance in your lives. Abundance can be experienced in food, money, relationships, energy, time, and material things. Maybe even speak about how you can share your fortune. Express gratitude for the abundance and take note of how it feels. Lock the feeling in so you can access it during winter when people often feel empty or depleted.

SEASONAL

Autumnal Equinox

INTENTION
Celebrate all that life has given you and use these gifts to fortify yourself for winter.

SOLO CEREMONY

TIME NEEDED
45 minutes

ELEMENTS
Items you have collected throughout the year: concert tickets, letters, items from Nature, souvenirs, playbills, and so on (see notes)

Harvest Box—a decorative box or container to collect the above items (see notes)

Paper and pen

Ribbon

The Autumnal Equinox marks the end of the productive growing season of summer and the beginning of the time to harvest and preserve the fruits of your labor for winter ahead. Autumn is associated with the West, sunset, and Wise Woman phase (see page 138). This ceremony captures and preserves the lessons of a busy year in a Harvest Box so that you can examine and work with them during the quiet months of winter.

STEPS

» Collect items that remind you of the year. Create or decorate a small box or container to capture the harvest of your year. This will be your Harvest Box.

» In order to feel grounded for this ceremony, play some music that reminds you of the year, such as a favorite playlist or album, and light some incense. Breathe deeply and feel the energy of the Earth around you vibrating with ripeness and perfection. This day is the last long inhale of fiery summer before Earth begins her descent toward winter. Everything is at its height on this day. Feel yourself full and brimming with all that has happened in the year so far.

» Spread your items from the year around you. Lay them out and marvel at all that has happened, the good and the bad. Pick up each item or written memory and place it in your Harvest Box. You may wish to write a note for each item, capturing a lesson or a thought about what happened. You do not have to go too deep right now; the energy is still too

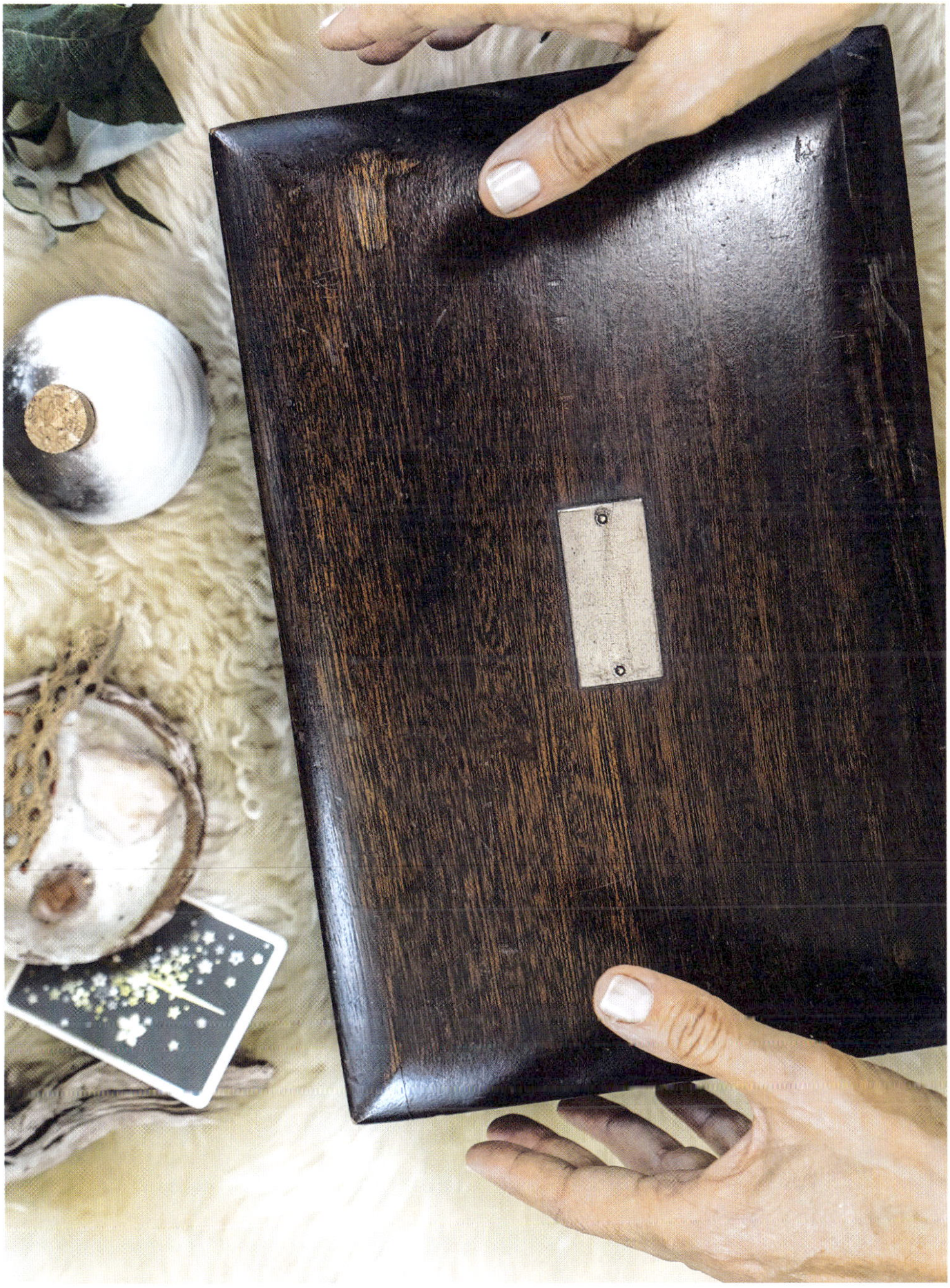

SEASONAL

high. For now, just capture and preserve. Go through each item and place it in the box, reflecting on your year to date.

» When you feel complete with your year's memories, close the box and tie it with a beautiful ribbon. It is a present to yourself, a time capsule of all the activity of the year. Store it in a safe place.

» Close the ceremony by breathing deeply and feeling the bounty of the year. Allow yourself to feel it all, high and low. Express gratitude for all that has happened so far, the good and the bad. Acknowledge the passing from the busiest time of year into a slower time. You are moving into sunset, when the day and the year slow down—not the deep sleep of winter, but a slower, quieter time.

》《

Notes: If you are not a collector, you can scroll through your calendar and write down some of the key or memorable events that have happened—both good and challenging—on individual pieces of decorative paper. You can even make small pieces of art from the events you're writing down, whether by calligraphy or sketches.

You can bring your Harvest Box to the New Year ceremony found on page 73 and use it to help you gather your wisdom lessons from the year.

Samhain

(DAY OF THE DEAD)

The Celts traditionally marked the end of their harvest season with the festival of Samhain (pronounced *sow*-in). Still celebrated in parts of the world, this ancient holiday is observed from sunset on October 31 to sunset on November 1, signaling the beginning of winter.

Modern-day Halloween (All Hallows' Eve) originated in the traditional celebration of Samhain. Remembering and honoring your ancestors can be a beautiful way to celebrate this potent portal of time when many cultures believe the veil between this world and the afterworld becomes thin, allowing us to access and be close to those who have passed.

This ceremony and altar practice can be performed on Samhain or closer to Thanksgiving, which also honors ancestors and gives thanks to those who came before us.

STEPS

» On October 31, or in the week leading up to it, determine the ideal location for an ancestor altar. It may be right in the middle of your home, where you and your family will pass it many times a day, or it might be in a quiet or sacred corner. This altar will represent your relatives who have passed away and give you a chance to have them close to you energetically. For inspiration, you can look up pictures of Día de los Muertos, a Mexican holiday with roots in Aztec culture, known for its elaborate ancestor altars.

(continues)

SEASONAL

INTENTION
Give thanks to and honor your departed ancestors; invite them to be close to you and to bring you comfort and wisdom.

SOLO OR FAMILY CEREMONY

TIME NEEDED
1–2 hours

ELEMENTS
Incense or candle

Sacred music

Items from favorite relatives who have passed on, such as jewelry, notes, clothing, linens, and instruments

Photos of ancestors

Items that represent the harvest: pumpkin, squash, apples (the fruit or the seeds), or the last flowers from your garden

Extra place setting

SEASONAL

» Before setting up your altar, ground yourself: Sit quietly, burn some incense or a candle, and play sacred music or songs that remind you of your ancestors. It can be meaningful to do this as a family, where you might sit in a circle and be quiet together. Breathe deeply and invite the spirits of your ancestors to join you in a circle. Say their full names out loud, noting the ancestors' lineage that each part of your name derives from, if any. You could invite each participant to name one ancestor they feel especially connected to.

» When you feel grounded, it's time to set up your altar. Do this intuitively. Take the items you have collected that represent your ancestors and arrange them however you like. You might start with a family tablecloth or linen on the surface, then place family heirlooms, photos of your ancestors, and items that represent the fall harvest as they feel right to you. Perhaps you have a corner of the altar for each part of the family, or perhaps there is a theme to your altar, such as weaving or food. Bring different ancestors to mind as you place the items, inviting them into your home through the symbolism of the altar. If you are doing this as a family, let each family member bring something to the altar.

» Once the altar is set, you can honor your ancestors for the gifts they have given you. Name as many of them as you can, and those you cannot call by name, you can call by description ("my mother's lineage from Mexico"). If you can name anything special about each part of your family, do so ("those who were musicians"; "the farmers who tended the land"). Let your ancestors know that you are honoring them with this altar and your presence, and invite them to dwell with you while the veil between the worlds is thin. You can speak thanks and blessings to them or write a letter or poem to place on the altar. Children can be invited to create a drawing for them.

» A beautiful tradition you can follow to honor ancestors is to set a place for them at your table. This can be during Samhain, at your Thanksgiving table, or through all of November. When you sit down to eat, you place a small portion of the meal on the ancestors' plate to honor them and invite them to be with you. You need only one plate for all of your ancestors. You may decorate their place setting with flowers, offerings, or notes.

» Use this time to acknowledge that the season is also changing from fall to winter. During winter, after the last harvest, the Earth quiets and slows down. Think of the gifts of the summer season and the fall harvest, and acknowledge that you are ready to move into winter, when the Earth will become darker. Welcome winter and the quiet contemplation that it will bring.

» You can decide to keep your altar up for just Samhain or for all of November. When you pass the altar, take a moment to remember and thank your ancestors. If you leave the altar up, be sure to tend to it, refilling the vase or freshening the flowers. Each member of the family could be invited to tend the altar for a day or a week. Once you are ready to put away your altar, lovingly take it apart and say a final thank-you to your ancestors.

SEASONAL

Thanksgiving

INTENTION

Give thanks for every thing, every being, and every force that brings abundance into our lives, and weave you and your loved ones together in gratitude.

GROUP CEREMONY

TIME NEEDED

30 minutes

ELEMENTS

Objects that represent your ancestors, such as jewelry, photos, or textiles

Family-favorite dishes and ancestral recipes to share

Printed decorative copies of the Haudenosaunee Thanksgiving Address (see notes)

Extra place setting

While Thanksgiving is always a day for giving thanks and expressing gratitude, it can be wonderfully expansive to give thanks and honor our connection to the natural world by reading aloud a prayer called the Haudenosaunee (*hoe-dee-no-SHOW-nee*) Thanksgiving Address. This prayer is used by the Haudenosaunee, a confederation of six Indigenous nations, to acknowledge the interconnectedness of all things and to unite communities in gratitude. It can work beautifully for your family or friends on Thanksgiving or anytime you gather.

STEPS

» Invite your guests to your feast and let them know that you will be celebrating community and the abundance of the Earth. Ask them to research the Indigenous communities who first inhabited the land you are occupying (see notes), so you can acknowledge their people during your ceremony. You may want to reflect on some of their traditions, history, or foods. You can also ask your guests to bring a family-favorite dish or make a recipe that has been passed down through generations.

» Set a beautiful table and invite guests to contribute objects from their lineage or ancestors to the table.

» Gather your group around your Thanksgiving table, or in a circle anywhere. Explain that this year you will honor the land and the forces of Nature in the way that many Indigenous people of the Americas did: by reading the Haudenosaunee Thanksgiving Address.

SEASONAL

» Invite each participant to read one section of the prayer. At the end of each section, the whole group will say in unison "now our minds are one."

» For a more personal ceremony, follow the prayer by inviting each participant to share what they are grateful for.

» Enjoy your traditional Thanksgiving feast, featuring foods your family cherishes. If it feels right, you can set an empty "ancestor plate" at the table, giving small portions of each dish to your ancestors with reverence and thanks.

Notes: You can find the Haudenosaunee Thanksgiving Address at shariboyer.com/thanksgivingprayer.

   Native-land.ca is a great source for researching Indigenous lands.

Haudenosaunee Thanksgiving Address
Words Before All Else

The People
Today, we have gathered and we see that the cycles of life continue. We have been given the duty to live in balance and harmony with each other and all living things. So now, we bring our minds together as one as we give greetings and thanks to each other as people.

Now our minds are one.

The Earth Mother
We are all thankful to our Mother, the Earth, for she gives us that we need for life. She supports our feet as we walk about upon her. It gives us joy that she continues to care for us as she has from the beginning of time. To our mother we send greetings and thanks.

Now our minds are one.

The Plants
Now we turn toward the vast fields of Plant life. As far as the eye can see, the Plants grow, working many wonders. They sustain many life forms. With our minds gathered together, we give thanks and look forward to seeing Plant life for many generations to come.

Now our minds are one.

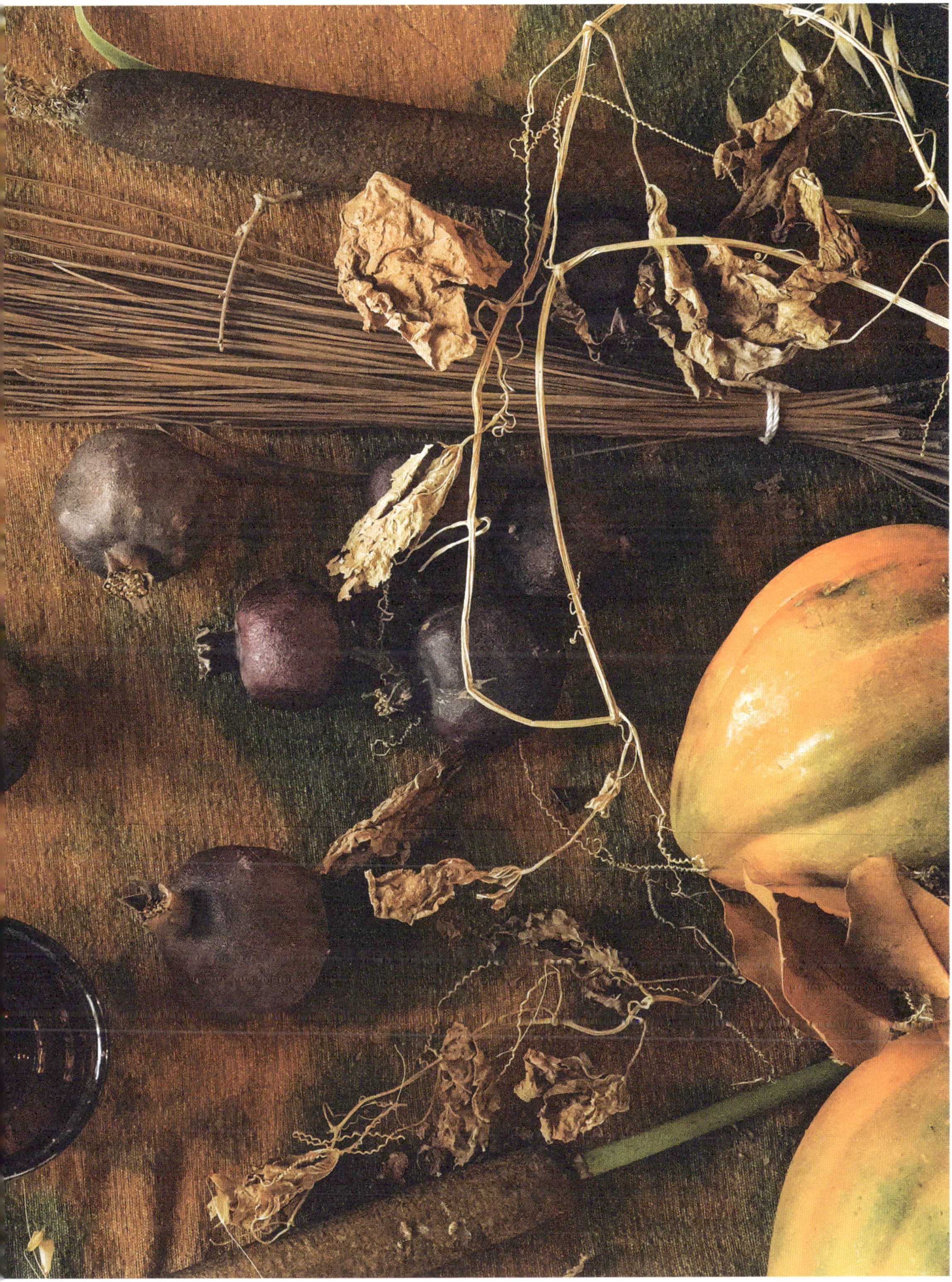

SEASONAL

Winter Solstice

INTENTION
Keep your inner flame stoked and alive during the darkness of winter.

SOLO CEREMONY

TIME NEEDED
30 minutes

ELEMENTS
Candles or fire source

Journal or paper/pen

Winter is the season of rest, when Mother Earth sleeps. Animals hibernate and trees lose their leaves to conserve energy for the future. We can take a hint from Nature and slow down to match her rhythms. Days are short, and our energy may be low. While we rest, it is also important to keep our inner flame alive. This is a simple ceremony to stoke your inner flame during the darkness. Perform this ceremony alone, as winter is naturally a more solitary time, giving you a chance to reflect inwardly.

STEPS

» Sit in front of a fire, or simply light a few candles.

» Find a seat where you can see and feel the outdoors. Winter is associated with the North and earth, so as you sit, feel your connection to the Earth and the soil, which sits dormant at this time of year. Close your eyes, breathe deeply, and imagine sending a tap root down from your root chakra (located at the base of the spine) through the floor and into the soil. Imagine the tap root descending down, down, down, through layers of soil, sediment, and rock. Let your tap root keep descending farther and farther down through the Earth until it reaches the inner molten core, where it is hot and fiery.

» Now imagine the fiery, molten heart of the Earth pulsing up through your tap root. Pull it up, through the layers of soil, through the floor, all the way to your body. Let the fire of the Earth enter your body through your root chakra and circulate throughout your body. See if you can feel the heat making its way through you. Let the heat settle in your body where you need it.

» Open your eyes and gaze at the candle or fire before you. Connect the feeling of heat inside your body with the fire. Lock the feeling in so that you can reconnect with it when you feel depleted or cold. You can say, "I feel the heat from the heart of Mother Earth alive inside me. I can access this heat at any time." Watch as the flames flicker and dance. Know that the fire inside you is also dancing and flickering at this time of year, even if more slowly.

» Finally, you may want to write down in your journal what seeds are germinating in the darkness. What lies dormant inside you but may grow and come alive as the Earth begins to wake up? Send energy to these seeds. You may have no idea what they will become, and that is totally okay; send them heat and energy anyway. Trust that they will germinate and begin to break ground when they are ready. Your job now is just to feed them and give them space to grow.

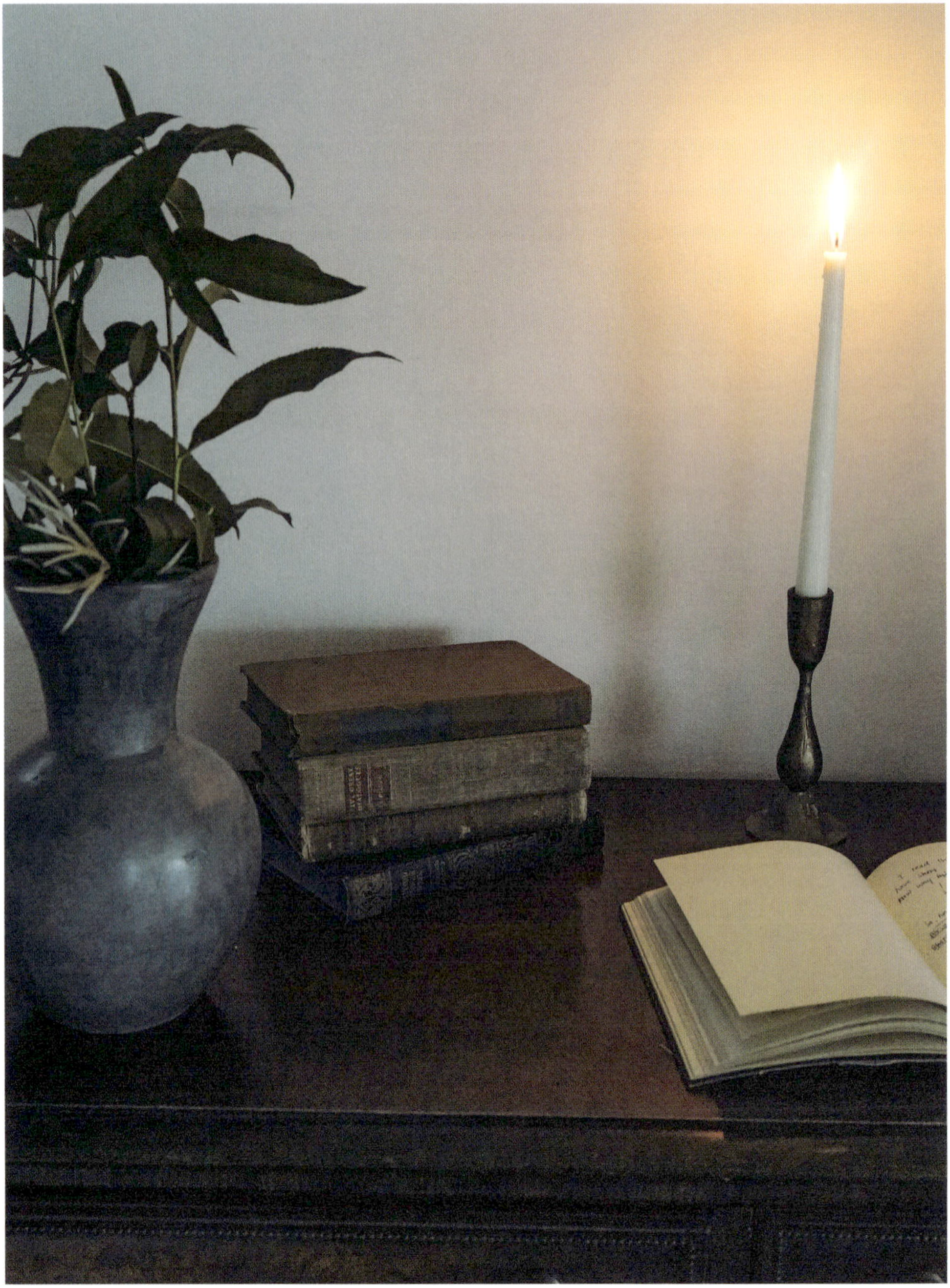

SEASONAL

New Year

The holidays bring a flurry of activity that can leave you depleted and stressed out. Then, New Year comes around, and there is pressure to create a New Year's resolution. When we move into a new year without properly digesting the prior year, we miss a chance to capture the year's lessons and release what is no longer needed.

This ceremony is perfect for performing on or around New Year's Eve. You can do this alone, with your family, or with some cherished friends.

If you created a Harvest Box on the Autumnal Equinox (page 60), you can use it in this ceremony to help remind yourself of some of the year's key activities.

STEPS

» Create a quiet and contemplative space. Make sure you have enough space around you to spread out some papers. If you have a group, form a circle, ensuring each participant has enough room to make a little circle around them within the bigger circle.

» Breathe, become centered, play sacred music, and light some blessing herbs or incense to encourage a contemplative state. If you are with a group, take three long, slow, deep breaths together.

» Take some index cards or paper and write a title on each that corresponds to an aspect of life you want to acknowledge. Some examples are: body, mental health, self, love/relationships/marriage, family/children, profession/job, dreams/

INTENTION

Gather the lessons from the year, process and release them, and enter the new year open and ready for what magic lies ahead.

SOLO OR GROUP CEREMONY

TIME NEEDED

1–2 hours

ELEMENTS

10–15 index cards or pieces of paper, pen

Sacred music

Blessing herbs or incense

Harvest Box, if available (from Autumnal Equinox ceremony)

Burning bowl or vessel

Candle or fire source

73

SEASONAL

goals/aspirations, finances, community, creativity, growth/learning, Nature, spirituality, home. You can create as many categories as you want to acknowledge. Place the index cards around you in a circle, where you are in the middle. If you have a Harvest Box, also place the items from the box around you.

» One by one, take each paper and reflect on that aspect of your life in the past year. On each page, answer these prompts: *What notable events happened? What changed? What did you learn? What are you releasing?* Write down all your thoughts and highlights, and at the bottom of each page, write down what you learned and what you are releasing. Move through each paper and aspect of your life.

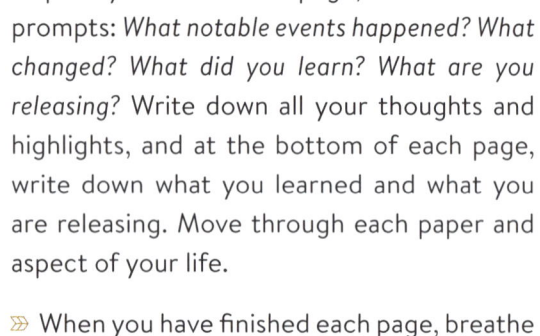

» When you have finished each page, breathe deeply and soak in the lessons and experiences of the year. Let them wash over you. Now, summarize the key lessons and takeaways from all the pages in your journal to serve as a summary of the year.

» If you are in a group, create time for each participant to share a few highlights or lessons from the year.

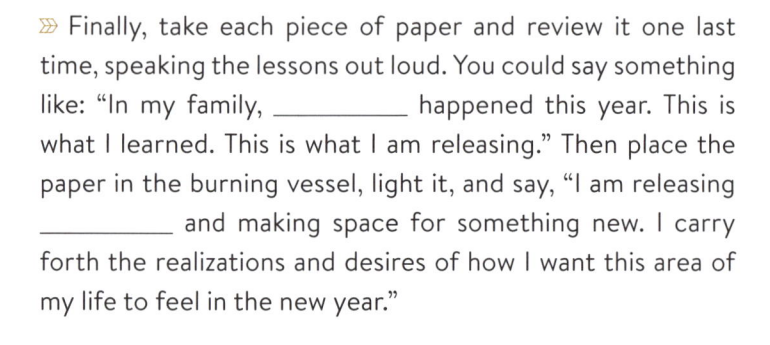

» Finally, take each piece of paper and review it one last time, speaking the lessons out loud. You could say something like: "In my family, _____ happened this year. This is what I learned. This is what I am releasing." Then place the paper in the burning vessel, light it, and say, "I am releasing _____ and making space for something new. I carry forth the realizations and desires of how I want this area of my life to feel in the new year."

SEASONAL

» Once you have burned all the papers, put away your items from the year. Sit in the middle of your now-cleared circle and reflect on the space you have created around you. Breathe in the promise of the new year, knowing you have gathered the lessons of the year and released all that is no longer needed.

» Celebrate with a meal, a walk, or whatever feels like self-care to you personally or to your group.

» In the coming days and weeks, take your time filling the space you have created with new projects, ideas, or resolutions. Allow the space to be void and pregnant with opportunity for a while. If you feel inspired and excited by new ideas, fantastic! Write down what is coming to you, dream about bringing the new projects to life, but pause a bit before rushing onward. This is the magic of winter—the quiet, the stillness, the void. You can metaphorically plant the seeds of your new idea, but know that seeds take time to germinate and blossom. The germination period may last through January and February until spring starts to activate something you planted in the darkness. Allow yourself to become comfortable with this not-knowing and see what begins to bubble up.

This ceremony was inspired by Marysia Miernowska, a folk herbalist and director of the School of the Sacred Wild. schoolofthesacredwild.com

CEREMONIES FOR LIFE EVENTS

To mark transitions and make meaning

Life events or rites of passage are some of the key times for holding ceremony. In many societies, each stage of life is marked with a ceremony, often witnessed by community members and elders, to signify that a change is taking place. Ceremonies focus on taking what is needed from the prior stage and gathering wisdom and the tools required for the next phase, pausing to mark meaning before moving on. When we skip these critical life stage transitions, we leave individuals to cope independently, with no guidance for how to behave in the next phase.

There are a few existing ceremonies that are meant to mark the transition to adulthood. These often have origins in traditional or religious practices, like the Jewish bar and bat mitzvah or the quinceañera in Latin cultures.

We also celebrate marriage with a ceremony. The next ceremony most people take part in is a funeral. We do not commemorate the stops along the way: the transition to menopause, becoming an empty nester, becoming a caretaker for an elderly parent, or becoming ill. Ceremony can be immensely healing and meaningful during these transitions, helping us to feel seen, supported, and held.

The ceremonies in this chapter are designed to offer ideas for life transitions. Some will celebrate familiar events (graduation, marriage, birthday) but with a new twist, and some will mark events you may not have thought to pause on (retirement, moving to a new home). Play and have fun; these are inevitable transitions, and marking them with your community makes them even more powerful.

CEREMONIES FOR

Celebrating Motherhood
80

Graduation
83

Mothers of Graduates
87

Coming of Age for Girls
94

Coming of Age for Boys
100

Remembering Home
106

Untraditional Birthday
109

Saying Goodbye to House and Land
114

Blessing a New Home
118

Commitment
122

Divorce
126

Retirement
130

Dealing with Illness
134

Menopause: Becoming a Wise Woman
138

Living Funeral
144

LIFE EVENTS

Celebrating Motherhood

INTENTION

Celebrate becoming a mother. Remind the mother-to-be that she is important and supported.

GROUP CEREMONY

TIME NEEDED

2 hours

ELEMENTS

Small pampering gifts for the mother-to-be, such as bath salts, an eye mask, slippers, lotion, pajamas, a crystal, or special tea

Flowers, pillows, and candles

Relaxing music

String or yarn

Favorite comfort foods to share

A basket to hold the gifts

Stationery, craft paper, pens

A Mother's Blessing, known as a Blessingway in the Diné tradition, honors the journey of pregnancy and becoming a mother as a rite of passage. A Blessingway focuses on the mother more than the baby and reminds the mama-to-be that she is supported and loved.

For this ceremony, invite the closest friends of the mother-to-be, along with trusted elders or women who have experience with motherhood. This event will be all about pampering and sharing wisdom. It can be celebratory and fun, like a traditional baby shower, but it centers on sharing wisdom with the mother-to-be rather than gifts for the baby.

Note: This ceremony can be adapted to celebrate anyone on the path to parenthood. Merely adjust the attendees and activities to suit the parent-to-be.

STEPS

≫ Invite those closest to the mother-to-be, letting them know that during your ceremony, you intend to pamper your friend and celebrate motherhood. Invite each participant to bring a small gift and a favorite comfort food for the meal. A good time to do this ceremony is one to two months before the baby's due date.

≫ Set up your space with flowers, pillows, candles, and relaxing music. You may wish to create an altar in your space with items honoring motherhood.

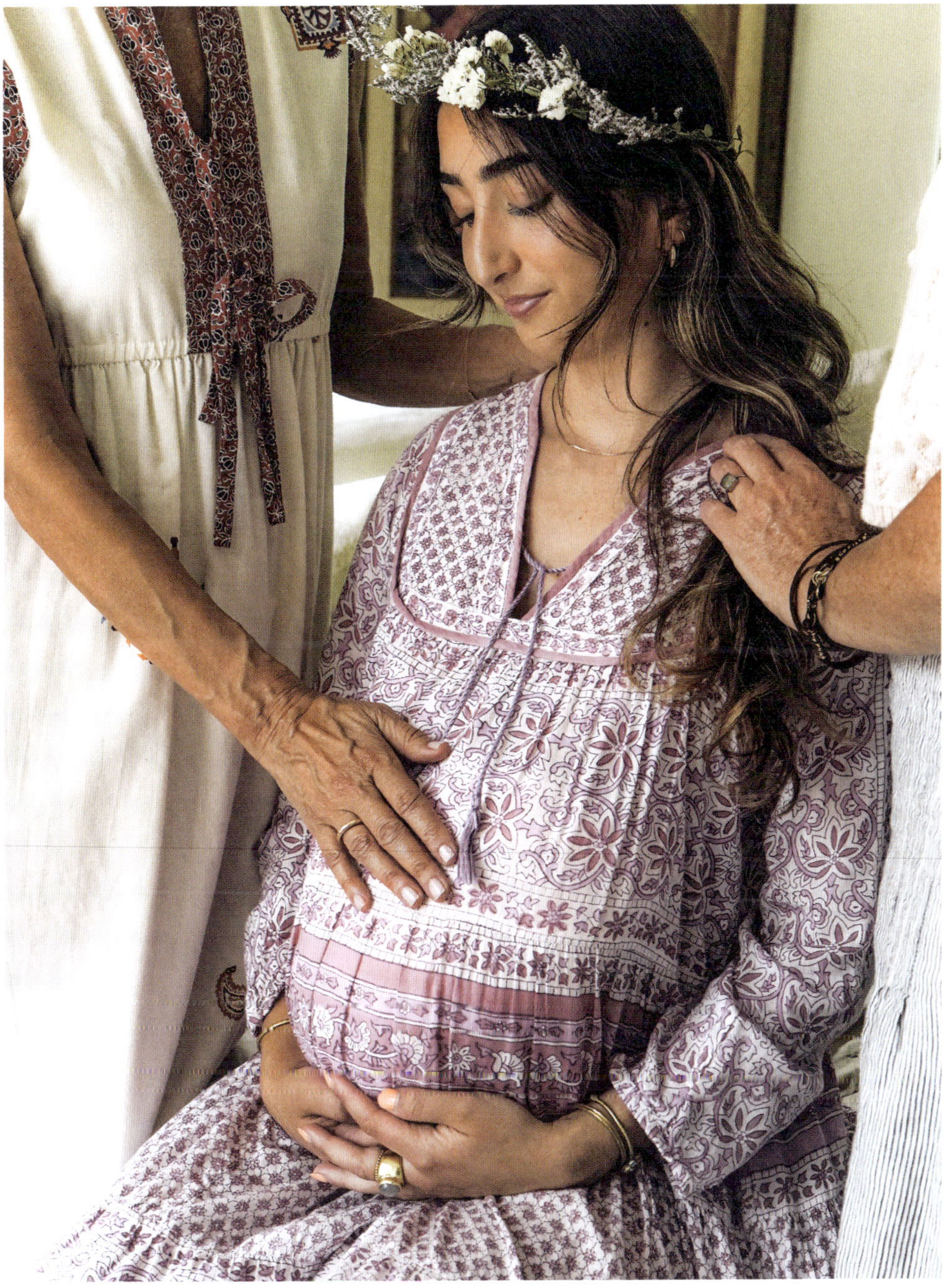

LIFE EVENTS

» When you are ready to begin, form a circle with all the participants. State your purpose. Invite each guest to greet the celebrant and tell her what they love about her or wish for her. You could say, "I wish you an easy transition into motherhood," or "I know you will make an incredible mother because you care so deeply about others."

» Take the string or yarn, cut a short piece, and tie it around your wrist. Tell the group that the yarn symbolizes the connection you each have with the new mother and that she has with her baby. Pass the yarn to another guest and let them tie a piece on their wrist. Pass the yarn around until all guests have made a bracelet. Turn toward the mother-to-be and let her know that the yarn connects you all and symbolizes the support you all have for her. Let her know that you each will wear the yarn as a reminder of her until the baby arrives.

» Now you can break into smaller groups and take turns speaking to the mother-to-be one-on-one. Set the mother-to-be up in a relaxing chair and pamper her with a foot massage or brush her hair. During this time, guests can write notes of wisdom or encouragement on the stationery and place them with the pampering gifts in the basket for mama to take home.

» When you have completed your notes and personally shared words of love and wisdom, gather for a meal together, enjoying the comfort foods you and your guests have prepared.

Graduation

This ceremony is meant to help a student of any age move from one grade or level to another by reflecting on the lessons from the past before transitioning to the new grade. It asks the student to use their intuition as well as listening to the wisdom of parents, teachers, or elders. This ceremony is wonderful when done in a group, such as with a class of students, but it can also be done alone with a parent or teacher.

STEPS

» Before the ceremony, invite the student to capture three favorite things about the past school year. This can be in a picture form (for younger students) or with words. This could encompass just the past year or cover a complete phase, such as all of middle school. If covering multiple grades, the student could summarize or draw each grade. Having some old assignments or photos on hand to jog the memory can be helpful.

» When you are ready for the ceremony, gather the group in one large circle with the student(s) seated in the middle. Have each student share their reflection with the group by either showing or explaining it. By doing this, the student is taking responsibility for their progress and not relying on outer validation.

» Next, a teacher can speak to each student, naming what progress they have seen in the student and what their strengths are. It can be gratifying to hear this from someone who knows the student well and to have strengths and

---

LIFE EVENTS

INTENTION
Create a feeling of being prepared for the next grade or phase of life.

GROUP CEREMONY

TIME
1–2 hours

ELEMENTS
Paper/pens

Photos and assignments from previous year or phase in school

Words or summary from a teacher

Words or summary from an older student

A bracelet, pen, certificate, or other symbol that signifies completion

Bridge, arch, or decorative line

LIFE EVENTS

accomplishments named out loud. Note that this occurs after the student has given their summary of the past, signaling that their intuition is as important as—or more important than—outside validation.

» If possible, have an older student speak to the graduate to let them know what they can expect in the next level and impart wisdom. They can say something like, "In lower school, your teacher told you what to do all the time, but in middle school, you will be responsible for more of your own decisions" or "It seems really hard at first, but it definitely gets easier." This helps the older student recognize their role as an emerging elder, and often, lessons from older students carry more significance for younger students than what a parent or teacher can offer.

» Next, present the student with the certificate or symbol of completion. Remind them that the certificate or symbol embodies all the learning they have achieved and carries the blessings and acknowledgment of the teachers, parents, and other students. This wisdom will always be available for the student to access each time they look at the certificate, bracelet, or other symbol.

» Have the student walk across a bridge or through an arch to signify moving from one level to the next. The act should be accompanied by words stating the transition, for example: "Once you cross through this arch, you will be a middle schooler, and you will be ready to take on the challenges and responsibilities of middle school." The teachers and parents should cheer for the student as they transition. If you do not have a bridge or arch, simply create a line on the ground, perhaps made from flower petals, and have the student jump or walk over the line.

(continues)

85

LIFE EVENTS

》 Finally, the student can state an intention that they have for the next grade. This could be how they want to act, what they want to learn, or simply a desire to be open to learning at a new level.

》 Close the ceremony by acknowledging the growth you have seen in the student and letting them know you can see that they are ready to move to the next level.

》 Celebrate the accomplishment of the student with a celebratory feast with their favorite foods.

> *This ceremony was adapted from the Manzanita School in Topanga, California, as described by Flora, a fifth-grade graduate who felt prepared for middle school after participating in this beautiful graduation ceremony.*

"It made me feel like there was respect and I was being held. I liked seeing people from the whole school, all the teachers and students; it felt like seeing a rainbow. It felt like fifth grade was then, but now I am going to be in sixth grade, so I could keep what I learned from fifth grade, but now I can use it in a new year. Drawing the picture of all the years helped me remember and see all the things that happened for the past few years—I remembered how much happened! When we burned part of the picture it meant I was releasing all the bad things that happened and keeping the good things. Walking over the bridge made me feel complete and ready for sixth grade; I could look back and see fifth grade behind me."

—FLORA

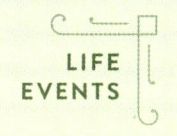

Mothers of Graduates

This ceremony will support mothers, parents, and caregivers who have a child leaving the home to attend boarding school, start college, or move into their own place. The impending departure of a child, whether it is a first child or the last, allows mama (or parent/caregiver) to clarify her wishes and intentions for her child and begin to think about what will fill the space that the child occupied in her life. This ceremony involves writing intentions that are then burned, a practice that allows the intentions to be released into the universe so that they can manifest.

The magic of this ceremony comes from witnessing each group member as you go through this transition together. After the ceremony you may choose to convene the group regularly to continue to envision what will fill the space for mama as the child leaves home. It can be easy to fill space with unimportant or unnecessary things, and having a circle that allows mama to focus on herself, her wishes, and her next phase can be incredibly potent.

The ceremony can be led by one person, or the prompts can be carried out by multiple participants in a coordinated effort.

LIFE EVENTS

INTENTION
Send your child into the world with wishes and call in your own dreams for the next phase.

GROUP CEREMONY

TIME NEEDED
1½ hours

ELEMENTS
Items that represent motherhood, such as a birth announcement, photo, baby rattle, blanket, shoe, or piece of clothing

Favorite food to share

Decorative textiles, flowers, and candles

Sacred music

Blessing herbs

Inspirational quote/poem

Journal or paper/pen

Fireplace or burning bowl/vessel

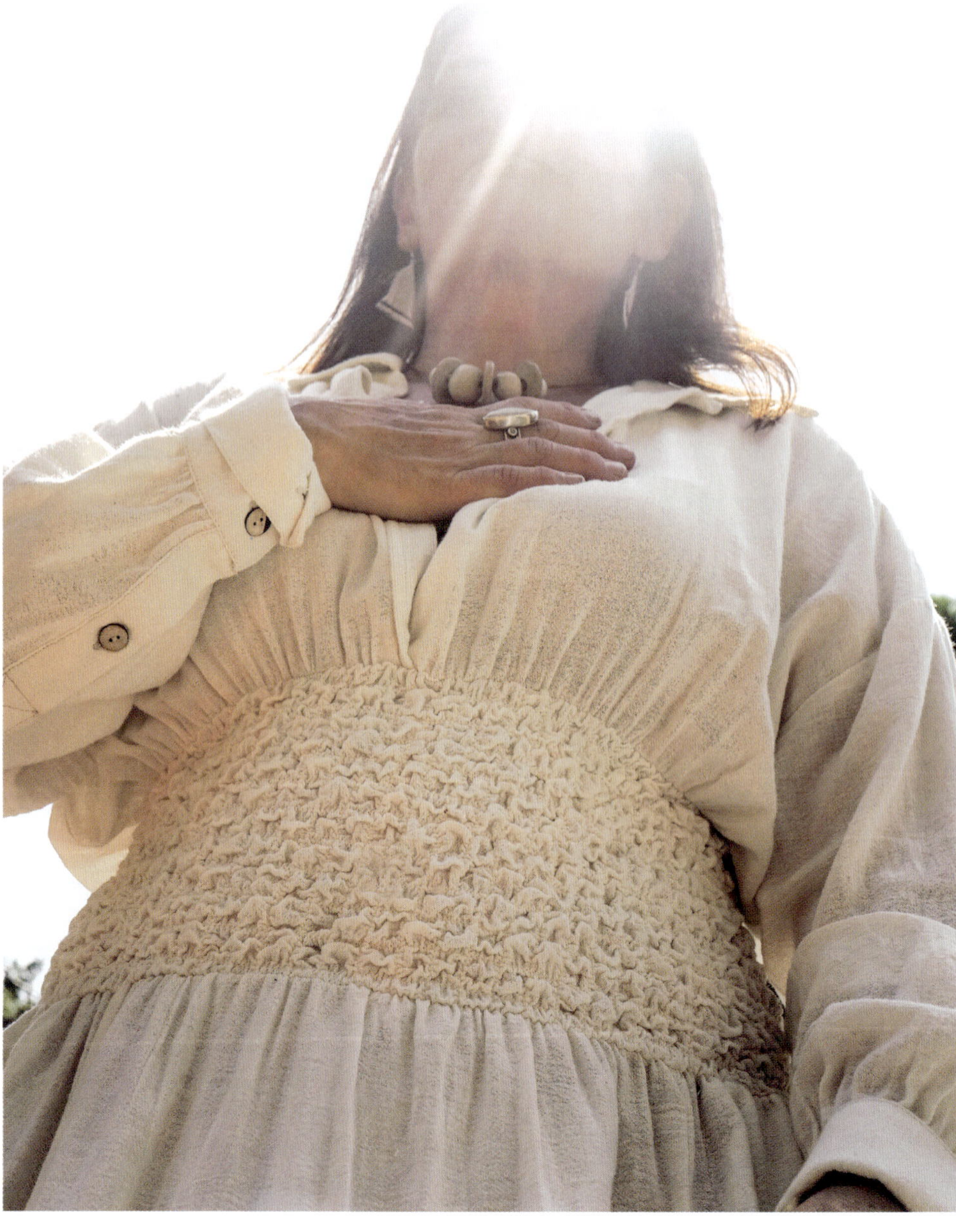

STEPS

≫ Send an invitation to your group, letting them know the intention of the ceremony and asking them to bring a special item representing motherhood for the altar and a dish to share for the celebration. Prepare a beautiful table for sharing a meal after the ceremony. Prepare your ceremony space in an inspirational, soothing, and private place. A garden, yoga studio, or backyard can be perfect. Ensure there is enough room for all participants to gather in a seated circle, with room to lie down if possible. Create an altar space in the middle of the circle using beautiful textiles, flowers, candles, and items representing motherhood or your children.

≫ When you are ready to begin, invite the participants to enter the ceremony space in silence and sit in a circle. Play sacred music and burn blessing herbs to help focus attention and create an introspective mood.

≫ Welcome the group and state the intention of your gathering. For example, you could say, "We are gathered today to create intentions for our children in their next phase and to create intentions for our own transitions from being active, day-to-day mothers into our next phase. Our intention is to support each other through these transitions and celebrate the joyous phases of our lives and all they have brought us and will bring us."

≫ At this point, you can have someone read an inspirational quote or poem or invite the participants to share how they are feeling. Many will feel grateful for the chance to take time for themselves, while others will feel scared, sad, excited, or all of the above.

(continues)

LIFE EVENTS

» Invite the spirit of all ancestors and the spirits of the land you are on to join your circle and lend their help on your journey. Once you have done this, state that your circle is cast, and you will have created a sacred circle that will only exist for this one moment in time.

» Invite participants to close their eyes, sit or lie down quietly, and breathe deeply. Invite them to feel the support of Mother Earth beneath them and connect to her energy. Remind participants to feel with their hearts and bodies, not with their minds.

» Guide your guests through a reflection on their child's life. Spend 5 to 7 minutes on this. You might say: "Remember the day you first saw your child. How did you feel? Were you excited? Scared? What were the first moments of meeting your child like? How did you feel as a mother? Now imagine your child on their first day of school. What did they look like? Were they scared, were you? Now imagine your child in middle school. How have they changed? Can you see them growing up? What is something your child loves? And finally, picture your child now. Hold an image of your child in your mind and feel your child in your heart."

» Invite each participant to cast her intentions for her child. Spend 5 to 10 minutes on this. You might say, "What hopes, dreams, and wishes do you have for your child? What do you want your child to carry forward with them as they move out into the world? What gifts can you give them? What helping guidance can you call for them?"

» Invite each participant to open their eyes when they are ready and write down their intentions for their child. They can write them on a piece of paper that will be burned to release their intention. They can also copy the intention on another piece of paper to share with the child.

(continues)

91

LIFE EVENTS

>> Invite anyone who wishes to share their experience or their intentions for their child to speak briefly but deeply to the group.

>> Now guide participants to turn their attention to themselves. Spend 10 to 15 minutes on this. You might say, "You created space in yourself and your life for your child, and now you are in a new stage as they move forward in their lives. What do you wish for, ask for, invite in? You can ask for anything. Listen with your whole body. Create an open space for something new or something that has been germinating to come through. It doesn't have to be fully formed or complete; just create the space and the invitation and see what comes. Remember that this is something for *you*, not your child, your partner, or your other children."

>> Invite participants to collect the messages that came through for them and write down what they have gathered in their journals. Have them settle on a phrase, mantra, image, or affirmation they can turn to over time to remind them of this space and this new beginning. For example, a mantra could be "I am ready" or "Nothing can hold me back."

>> Invite participants to share what they received.

>> Recount for participants the special work you have just done together. You might say: "Today, we have created intentions for our children and sent our intentions for them out to the universe. We have also prepared ourselves for our next phase. We have opened up space and invited in new

energy and ideas. We are potent with creativity and possibility. We have woven together with mothers of all time, joined them in our wishes for our children, and asked them for guidance and strength for ourselves as we move forward."

» Thank each person for participating, being bold and open, and for their love. Let everyone know that the circle will end but the work done during your ceremony will stay with each of them. Remind each participant to repeat the mantra or affirmation they have settled on to bring them back to the sacred space of your circle. You might say, "Our circle is open but never broken. We are woven together in our motherhood and our transition. Our support for each other will last as we move out into the world. You can draw on the strength that we have created together today at any time by repeating the mantra or affirmation you created today."

» Finally, together you will release your intentions for your children by burning them and asking the fire to carry them out into the world. Have each mother stand next to a fireplace or large burning bowl. One by one, read the intention aloud and place the paper in the bowl. Light the papers on fire, and watch the smoke carry your intentions into the world.

» Invite the group to the prepared table to enjoy a refreshment or meal together while you integrate the healing created during the ceremony.

LIFE EVENTS

Coming of Age
FOR GIRLS

INTENTION
Usher a girl into young adulthood, honoring her uniqueness while giving her a sense of being supported and seen.

GROUP CEREMONY

TIME NEEDED
3–4 hours, depending on number of participants

ELEMENTS
Letters or talismans for the honoree from each participant

Vessel of Care: a decorative container to collect gifts for the honoree

Objects for self-care, such as tea, candles, or a journal

Cushions

(continues on opposite page)

Young women reaching the threshold of adolescence in Western culture often lack adequate support and way-showing during this pivotal developmental stage.

This ceremony invites you to create a Circle of Care—a group of trusted advisers who are committed to helping a young woman through this phase, bestowing wisdom, love, and guidance. Ideally, these women would be an intergenerational group composed of older teens, young adults, older adults, and elders.

This ceremony can be performed at any significant moment in a girl's life, such as the onset of puberty, the transition to high school, or an important birthday. Many religions and cultures celebrate the transition from girlhood to young adulthood at age thirteen (bat mitzvah in Judaism), fifteen (quinceañeras in Hispanic culture), sixteen (Sweet Sixteen in the United States and Canada), or eighteen (debut in the Philippines). Choose the time that feels right for your young woman and your Circle of Care. Make sure that your celebrant is aware of the ceremony and has some say in its design so she feels comfortable—but it can be fun to keep some surprises for her as well. This should be a day of celebration and wisdom passing.

Note: This ceremony and the following Coming of Age for Boys (page 100) can be adapted and used for individuals of any gender identity or expression.

STEPS

» Send a beautiful invitation or make a personal phone call to the women you wish to include, letting them know what role you would like them to play in the ceremony. Give the ceremony details and ask them to write a note to the honoree, expressing anything they wish to reflect to her about her growth and any wisdom they would like to share with her. Suggest they bring a small item of significance to give the honoree as a talisman of their love. If they cannot attend but want to be a part of it, they can send you an item for the ceremony.

» Prepare a special box or basket to serve as a vessel for gathering the letters and talismans. You may want to decorate the container and add self-care items such as special tea, bath soak, a candle, or a notebook.

» On ceremony day, create a beautiful circle with cushions for attendees around a central altar. If possible, plan your ceremony to be enacted at a place near a body of water—at a beach, alongside a riverbank, or near a lake—as the element of water is intimately connected to the womb space, and integrating this element in a significant way will be supportive of the ceremony. The altar can be composed of objects of beauty that resonate for the young woman being honored. Include items that represent each of the elements—earth, air, water, fire. Suggestions include flowers or soil for the earth, beeswax candles for fire, a bowl of water, and a feather to honor the air.

» When you are ready, gather the group. Burn some herbs or incense, such as sage or lavender, to welcome attendees and set a sacred tone. Invite each person to enter the sacred space and prepare for the ceremony. When the young woman

---

LIFE EVENTS

Beautiful objects that resonate with the initiate

Items representing the four elements: earth (flowers, soil), air (feather), water, and fire (candle, preferably beeswax to evoke harmony with the hive)

Herbs or incense for burning, such as lavender

Flower crown or bouquet, plus loose flower petals (preferably rose)

Sacred music

Crystal or special shell to serve as a talking piece

Sage leaves

Paper/pen

Wisdom Gift—a beautiful piece of jewelry, a scarf, book, or other object that will represent young adulthood, usually from mother to daughter

Favorite foods of the honoree's to share

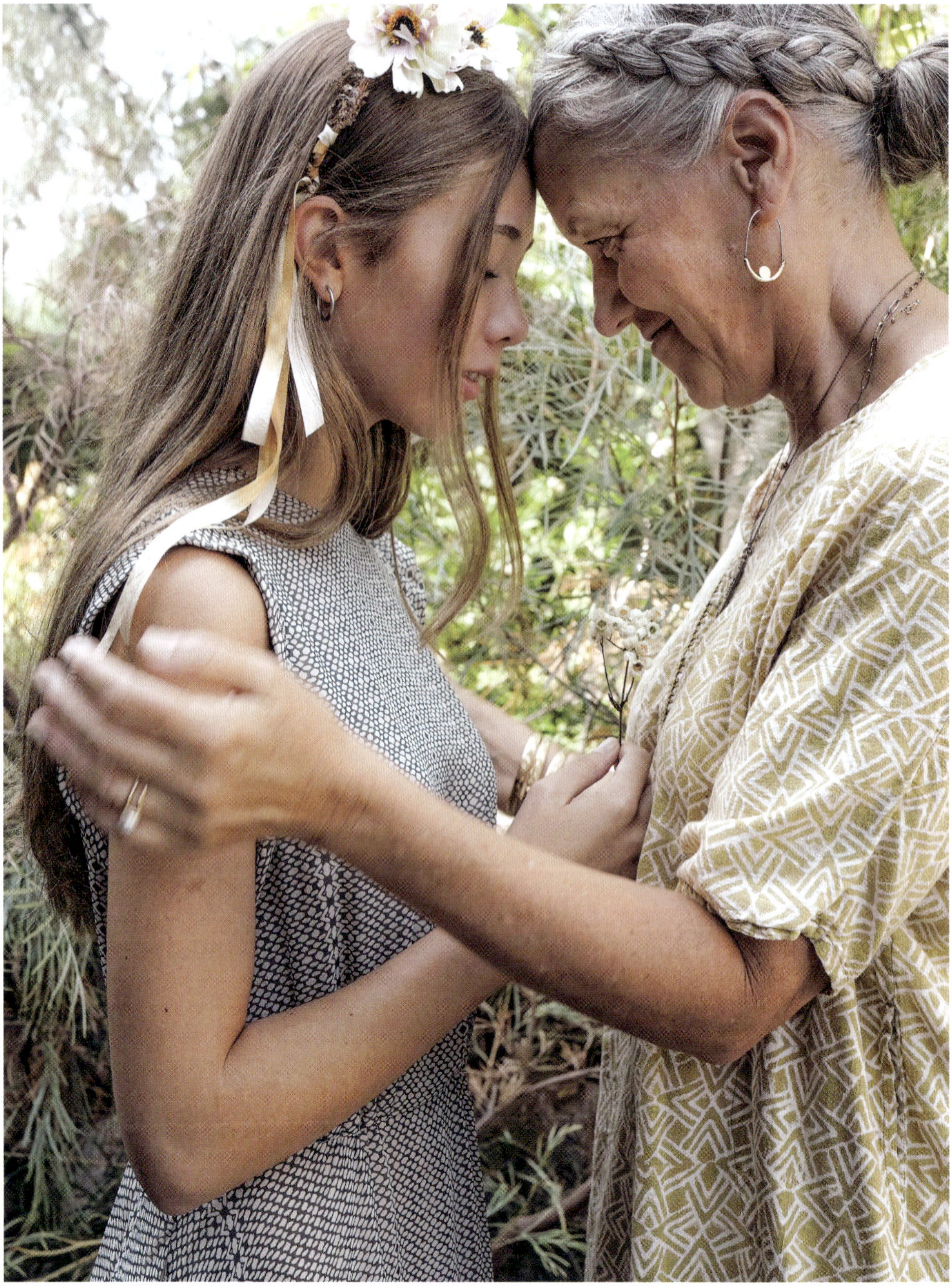

enters, place a flower crown on her head or give her a bouquet of wildflowers to hold.

» Begin the ceremony by playing sacred music and inviting all participants to be fully present. Invite the four directions and their elements (East/air, South/fire, West/water, North/earth) and the spirits of all mothers to join the circle. Invite the ancestors of the initiate to be present for her. Let all the participants know that you are in a sacred circle, outside of time, and that what you create during this ceremony will take place only once but will live within each of you forever.

» Honor the initiate by telling a brief account of her childhood journey and make it clear that this ceremony is intended to honor her growth and maturation and to welcome her into the next phase of her life. Make it clear that as with all passages, this is a process, and that as she transitions into womanhood she is encouraged not to rush this stage of growth but rather to enjoy those activities and delights that connect her to her youth while also being encouraged to see herself in a new light. Encourage her to explore her change and maturation, authentically following new interests, attitudes, and activities that may call to her. Invite her to listen to her inner wisdom.

» Now invite each of the women gathered to describe a quality of the initiate's that they admire. Designate a crystal or shell to serve as the talking piece, allowing only the person holding it to speak. Each woman can share a story of when they witnessed this quality expressed or recount a significant memory they have of her. Once each speaker is complete, they should pass the talking piece on to the next person.

» Welcome the initiate to share how she is feeling at this time. Assure her that this is a safe space for her to self-express freely, without judgment, and be witnessed, loved, and supported. Invite her to share from her heart. This is also a time for the initiate to share anything that she is ready to release or let go of: these could be habits she's ready to change, self-limiting beliefs that she'd like to let go of, or old thoughts or feelings that are no longer serving her.

» Next, invite the initiate to burn single sage leaves over the candle to symbolize what she is releasing, for example, "I release my fear of traveling outside my home without my family" or "I release my need to be perfect and always know the answer." Alternatively, she could write or draw what she is releasing and burn the paper with the words or symbols. Once she has done this, have her add some rose or other flower petals to the body of water as a symbol for the space created through the release being filled with loving energy.

» Share with the initiate the importance of self-love and self-care as she navigates adolescence and moves into young adulthood. This is a beautiful time to perform an act of self-care for the young woman as the participants each share their favorite ways to shower themselves with love and care. If you are celebrating a first menses, make it clear to the initiate that this time of the month is when she may feel more emotional, sensitive, and receptive and that this is to be treasured and honored. You can give her a hand or shoulder massage, prepare a footbath for her, or brush and braid her hair as she listens to what the attendees each share.

» Have each attendee share something they wish they had known about adolescence, a piece of wisdom, and how they would like to support her through her transition to young adulthood. Each attendee speaking from the heart will create a woven prayer of protection for the honoree. Participants

LIFE EVENTS

can present the young woman their gift as they share, explaining why they have chosen this item. Each item becomes infused with the prayer and wish of the giver and will hold that energy for the honoree moving forward.

≫ The initiate can now be presented with the Wisdom Gift you have chosen for her—this can be a piece of jewelry with symbolism associated with the young woman, such as her birthstone or a piece of family jewelry. It can also be a book, scarf, or anything that represents adulthood. As you present the item to her, you can say, "With this gift, I acknowledge the transition from child to young adult. I witness your transition and commit to serving as your guide and support."

≫ Invite the initiate to share from her heart, if she feels comfortable doing so, with a word, phrase, or wish for herself in young adulthood. It can be powerful to also invite her to make a pledge or commitment to her community.

≫ Close the ceremony with a blessing, song, or poem. Remind the initiate that even though the participants will disperse after the ceremony, the circle of care and guidance will always surround her spiritually.

≫ Celebrate with a feast of the honoree's favorite foods!

This ceremony was inspired by Eve Gaines of Rituel, a ceremony space and collective in Malibu, California. rituellife.com

LIFE EVENTS

Coming of Age
FOR BOYS

INTENTION

Initiate a boy into young adulthood and impart wisdom from elders. Create a circle of trusted advisers to whom the young man can turn when needed.

GROUP CEREMONY

TIME NEEDED

4 hours–2 days

ELEMENTS

Wisdom Journal— a beautiful blank book or journal and pens

A gift for the boy from each adult (such as a pen, a book, a piece of sports equipment for his favorite sport, or an heirloom)

Camping gear

Campfire or other fire source (such as candle or lantern)

A symbol of youth from the boy (an old toy, trophy, baby blanket, photo, etc.)

Moving from adolescence into adulthood is one of the most important transitions that anyone will make in their lives. In traditional cultures, this transition is marked with events and challenges that help the youth gain the skills and wisdom necessary to succeed in the next phase and understand their own unique gifts.

In much of Western culture, we sorely miss these rites of passage, and we should aim to provide more support and guidance as our children transition into young adulthood.

This ceremony is ideally organized by a mentor in a boy's life: a father, uncle, friend of the family, or older brother. However, wisdom comes from many voices, so if there is someone else better suited to organize or lead this ceremony, then by all means invite them in.

This ceremony aims to impart life wisdom, love, and guidance to a young boy that they can use as they move into adulthood, create a trusted circle of advisers, and help them recognize and believe in their gifts. The suggestion is for a weekend camping trip, which serves two purposes: It removes the group from daily life and helps the group connect to Nature. If a weekend or camping is not feasible, simply modify to an afternoon in the woods or a park. What is important is setting aside the time and place outside of the norms of daily life.

Note: This ceremony and the previous Coming of Age for Girls (page 94) can be adapted and used for individuals of any gender identity or expression.

STEPS

» Long before this ceremony takes place—possibly a year or two—let the boy know about it and its purpose. You can begin the conversation around the fact that one day, he will move into adulthood with a special ceremony. You can decide that it will take place on a particular day, such as his thirteenth or fourteenth birthday or the first full moon of summer. Whatever you decide, make sure to begin discussing this special event long before it actually happens so everyone is prepared and excited. Talking about it in advance also allows you to work out any worries or fears that may come up and to prepare your participants. This can be discussed as a family, or the person organizing the ceremony can lead the discussion.

» Decide who in the boy's life could serve (or already serves) as a special adviser to the boy. Someone who knows him well, cares about him, and is willing to commit to a lifelong relationship of trust. You can ask just one other person or many, but usually two or three is a good number and will not be overwhelming. Let the members of this group, the Wise Council, know what you have in mind long before you start your ceremony. Invite each of them to be an adviser to the boy, and explain what it will entail, so there are no surprises. Give them some time to formulate how and what they'll choose to share.

» Purchase or make a blank journal that will serve as the Wisdom Journal. This journal will be filled with advice and wisdom from each member of the Wise Council, as well as the young boy's own observations and lessons.

(continues)

LIFE EVENTS

» Invite the members of the Wise Council to join you for the initiation weekend. Be sure to clearly state your intention for the weekend as a rite of passage into adulthood. Plan a weekend full of Nature-based activities—hiking, fishing, climbing—whatever suits your group. Plan group meals and assign each member of the party a meal or some ingredients to bring. Ask each adult to think about what one piece of advice for life they would give, along with a small gift, a token of adulthood. You may wish to make a policy about the use of phones and devices during the weekend and let participants know in advance. Choose your camping or gathering spot and make your reservations.

» When your ceremony date arrives, treat it with care. Gather your camping gear, delicious meals and snacks, games, sports equipment, and whatever else you need. Be sure to bring the Wisdom Journal and some pens, and the advisers can bring their gifts for the young boy. When you arrive, convene as a group and gather in a circle to state your intention. You can say, "We are here to mark the passage of _____ into adulthood. We are the Wise Council of Elders who commit to advising and witnessing _____'s passage into adulthood." Be sure to state the young boy's name, and you can also acknowledge any lineage or ancestors (such as deceased grandfathers) and invite them to join the weekend in spirit. Give an overview of the activities and responsibilities of the weekend.

» During the weekend, invite each adult to find some time alone with the celebrant to share what they see as a unique strength or gift of the young man, along with a piece of advice. They can assure him that they will always be available to speak with and listen to him. They may even want to set up a cadence for such a connection, such as a monthly call, hike,

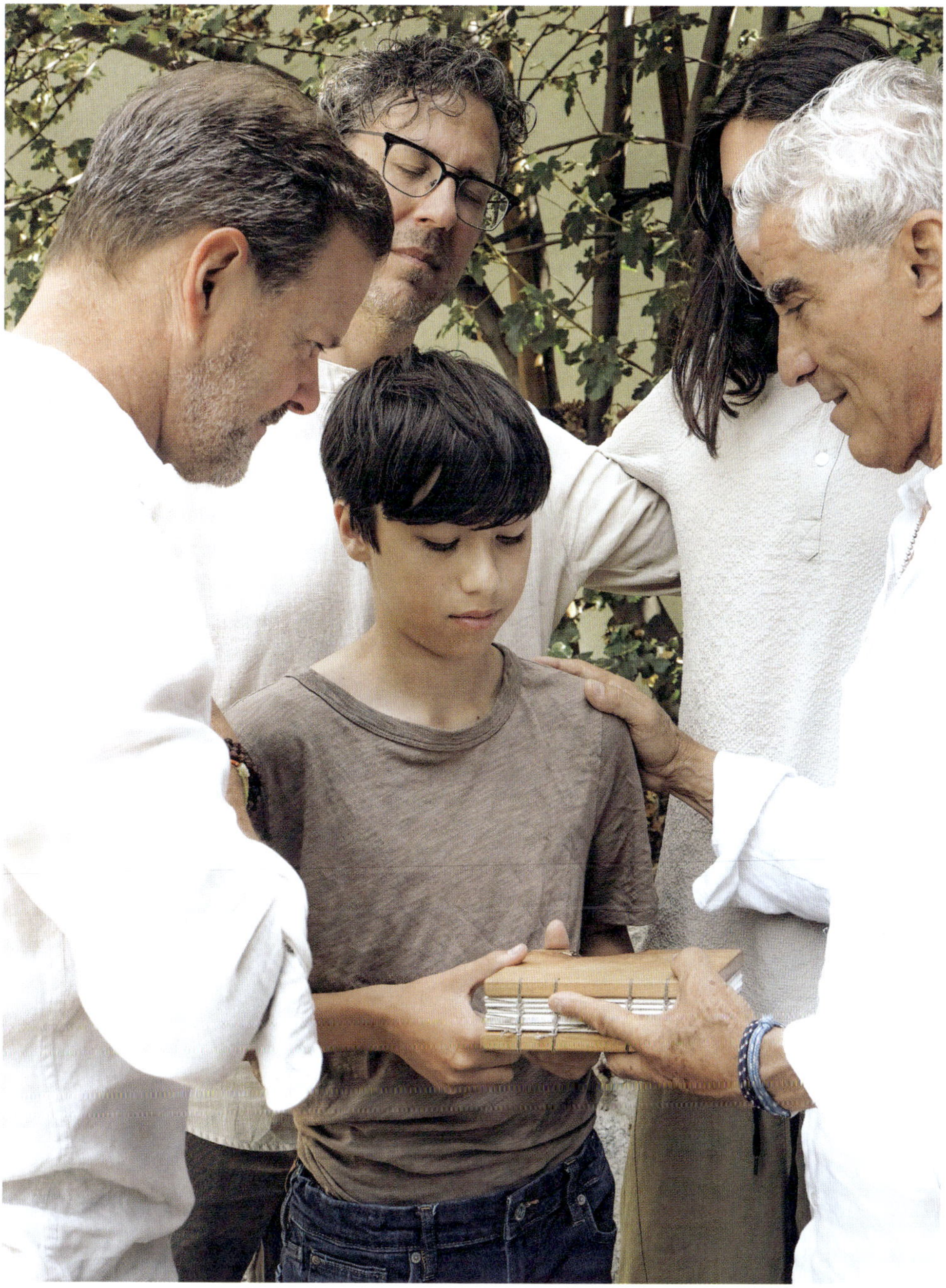

LIFE EVENTS

lunch, or favorite activity. Other activities can be planned based on what the young boy likes to do or around activities that demonstrate skills needed in adulthood, such as perseverance, patience, strength, teamwork, planning, connection, and self-care. The adults should record their advice in the Wisdom Journal sometime during the weekend.

》 The heart of the weekend will be the ceremonial "letting go" of youth. This can start by the men reflecting on and celebrating their own youth by telling stories of their younger years. Do this over a campfire or meal. The council can regale the young boy with things they did—good and bad, wise and foolish. The members of the council who have known the boy his whole life can tell kind, non-embarrassing stories of his boyhood that they want him to remember and celebrate. Invite the initiate to share his own stories as well. Perhaps someone captures these memories in the Wisdom Journal. When you have completed the trip down memory lane, invite the young boy to place the feeling of these memories in the special object from youth that he brought with him. Let him know that these memories will always exist in your hearts and in this object and that now it is time to let go of youth and move into young adulthood. You can symbolize the letting go of youth by burning a piece of paper with a wish for the future written on it, releasing it to the universe. Another way to mark the transition would be to blow out a candle or lantern or put out the campfire.

≫ The final step is to receive the young man into adulthood. Create a circle around him. State that the adults present are willing to witness and stand up for him as he matures into adulthood and pledge to serve as counsel throughout his life. Present the Wisdom Journal to the initiate, letting him know that it holds collected wisdom from the Wise Council, but also will serve as a place to record his own wisdom, emotions, and thoughts through the years. Invite him to consider the long line of ancestors he hails from and invite the wisdom of those ancestors to be present. Go around the circle and have each adult witness the young man and pledge to stand by him. They can present their gifts at this time. When you have completed the circle, invite the initiate to make a commitment to the group. He might say, "I pledge to honor this council by always speaking the truth," or "I pledge to make my community better." Once he has spoken his commitment, he may step out of the center of the circle and join the circle of adults.

≫ A celebration is in order! This can be a meal, a hike, a song, or anything that suits your group.

≫ The organizer can check in with the Wise Council members from time to time to see if they are keeping their commitment to the young adult. It can also be helpful to set up established check-in times, such as on a birthday or the anniversary of the ceremony.

LIFE EVENTS

Remembering Home
FOR WHEN A CHILD LEAVES THE NEST

INTENTION

Give a child an accessible feeling of home to call on wherever they are.

FAMILY CEREMONY

TIME NEEDED

45 minutes

ELEMENTS

Items that represent home for your child, such as soil from the land, pictures, a talisman, childhood objects, a piece of holiday decor, letters, awards, or a diploma

Candle

Incense or blessing herbs, such as copal, cedar, or pine

(continues on opposite page)

Leaving home is an enormous step for children, whether they are going away for college or attending summer camp for a few weeks. It can cause anxiety not only for the parents but also for the child. This ceremony is intended to help children "lock in" the feeling of home and remind them that they can connect to that feeling at any time, wherever they are. It serves as a beautiful transition for both those staying and those leaving.

STEPS

» Find a space that is quiet and protected. This can be a special place in the home or outside, but it should be at the primary residence. Set up a circle or space where your family or group can sit comfortably together. Make a small altar in the middle or near your circle with the items you have gathered that represent your home. Lay the altar with intention, love, and presence. Be sure to have the child include an item that reminds them of home. Light the candle, burn some blessing herbs or incense, and play the chosen music. You can also include items representing the four elements and place them in this order:

- » *East—air*
- » *South—fire*
- » *West—water*
- » *North—earth*

LIFE EVENTS

» Gather as a family together in a circle, including pets if it feels right. Breathe deeply together, and hold hands if you like. State your intention. You can say, "Today we are going to invite the feeling of home into our bodies so that we can hold it there even when away."

» Breathe deeply, imagining that you are breathing in the home around you. Invite each participant to focus on the feeling of home. What does it feel like in your body? In your mind? What does it smell like? Once the feeling of home is present, invite the child to lock this feeling into their body, their heart, and their mind. Guide them to consciously hold the feeling of home inside themselves. Maybe a word or phrase or image comes up that can be a touch point to home. Capture this word or feeling on paper or in your mind and know that recalling the word or phrase at any time will allow the feeling of home to become present. Take 15 to 20 minutes to allow these feelings to arise and settle around you. Write down the words, phrases, or images that come to you. For example, words that might arise are "safety, comfort, good food, memories, my favorite things."

» Present a small box full of items to remind your child of home and where they come from: photos, little mementos, special items representing your home or city, words of love, words of wisdom. Give them the box and remind them that home will always be with them. Remind them that anytime they engage with the items in the box, they will be connected to home and connected to the feeling of home that they carry with them in their body. They can add the word or phrase they created to the box. It is also nice to include something from the land your home is on, like a rock, dried flower, or leaf.

» Finally, invite the person leaving to think about anything they want to let go of: anything that is not serving them

Playlist of your child's favorite music

Items representing the four elements (optional): air (feather), water, fire (candle), earth

Paper and pen

Home in a Box: small box or bag containing reminders of home

LIFE EVENTS

anymore, or will not serve in the new place. Guide them to identify and release it. They can also write down something they want to leave behind and burn the paper to release it.

» You can end by offering a wish for the child, for example, "I wish for you to be brave and present while at college, and to know that you can connect with us when you need to." A sibling might say, "I wish that you will let me use your bike while you are gone and know that I will take great care of it." Go around the circle and offer your wishes to the person leaving.

» The child leaving can also offer a wish or a prayer to the rest of the family.

» When the ceremony is complete, celebrate by enjoying a meal of favorite family foods or an activity or game that you all enjoy.

Untraditional Birthday

Birthdays are often celebrated with joy when we are young and then approached with some dread as we age, driven by our youth-obsessed culture. In other cultures around the world, age is celebrated and marks a time to have gratitude for all of the abundance in your life.

This ceremony is an opportunity to mark your birthday by celebrating your life, including the people most important to you or those who contribute to your life. It is a chance to throw a gratitude party for those you love most. Instead of gifts given to you, you will celebrate the gifts of your life, your chain of ancestors, your place of residence, and your abundance. By celebrating others on your special day, you are acknowledging that you cannot exist without the connection to and love of your community.

STEPS

» Invite your most beloved friends and family to a meal in celebration of your birthday. Let them know that you do not want them to bring a gift, that instead you will be "reversing" on this birthday and celebrating them. You can invite them to bring a dish if you like, or you can prepare all the food yourself, order takeout, or even have your ceremony at a restaurant—but a home celebration can be particularly nice.

» Set the table with your best dishes and flatware. This is a time to celebrate! Take out the china, crystal, and good linens. Place flowers and items from Nature on the table. If you like, you can set one place at the table to represent your ancestors or anyone you love who can't be present.

(continues)

LIFE EVENTS

INTENTION
Celebrate all the people and things that make your life blessed and wonderful. Give thanks (and gifts) to those you care about most.

GROUP CEREMONY

TIME NEEDED
2 hours

ELEMENTS
A thoughtfully prepared or ordered dessert

Flowers and other items from Nature

Extra place setting

A gift for each participant (optional)

LIFE EVENTS

》 When you are ready, invite everyone to sit at the table. Begin by letting everyone know that they are there because they are your most beloved, those who make your life beautiful and full of meaning. Let them know that on your special day you want to shower with gratitude those who support you. You can say something personal to each guest, such as what you most love about them or what they bring into your life. If you have a small gift for each guest, deliver it as you speak. You can also honor everything your ancestors have made possible for you. You can name ancestors by name and give thanks to those whose names you do not know.

》 If it feels good to you, thank the elements of Nature that support you, all the gifts that make you who you are, and all of the abundance in life. You can say things like "I am grateful for the amazing job that I have and my coworkers who support me. I am grateful for the abundance of food that graces my table. I am grateful for my healthy body." Name the big things and the little things.

》 When you have finished with your gratitude, if it feels comfortable, you can invite your guests to toast you in return. Maybe give them a prompt: "Would you honor me by telling me what I bring to your life or how I support you?" Or "What is my best trait?" Or "What is one gift of my life that I haven't noticed?" Then, sit back and bask in the love and abundance flowing to you. Allow yourself to truly open up and feel the sentiments being expressed. Asking for feedback or praise can be uncomfortable, but remember that these are your most beloved friends, so let them tell you how much they love and admire you. Let it be their gift to you!

》 Finish the meal with a delicious dessert and invite all to taste the sweetness of life and of community. Literally, ingest and digest the sweetness of life together.

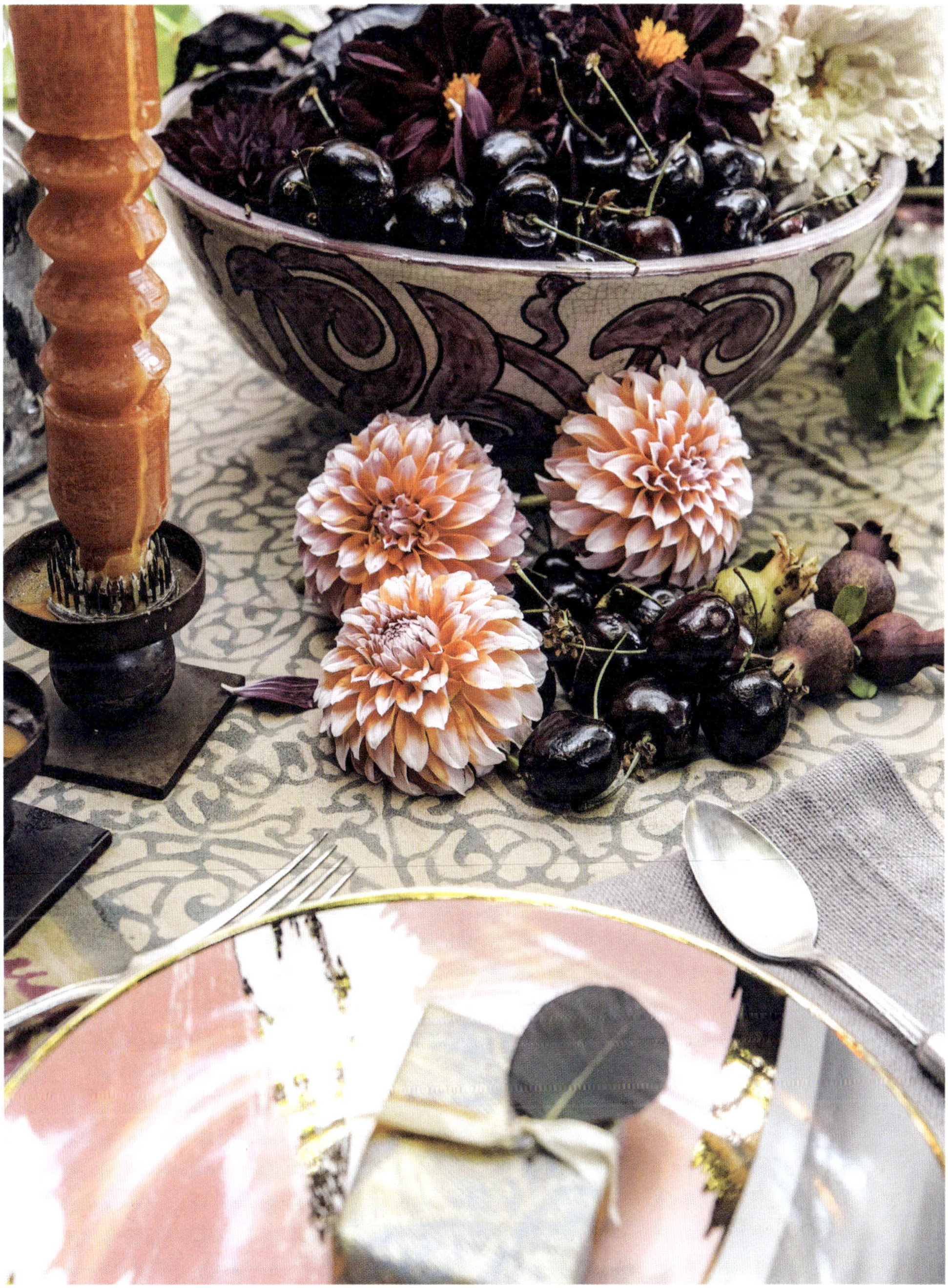

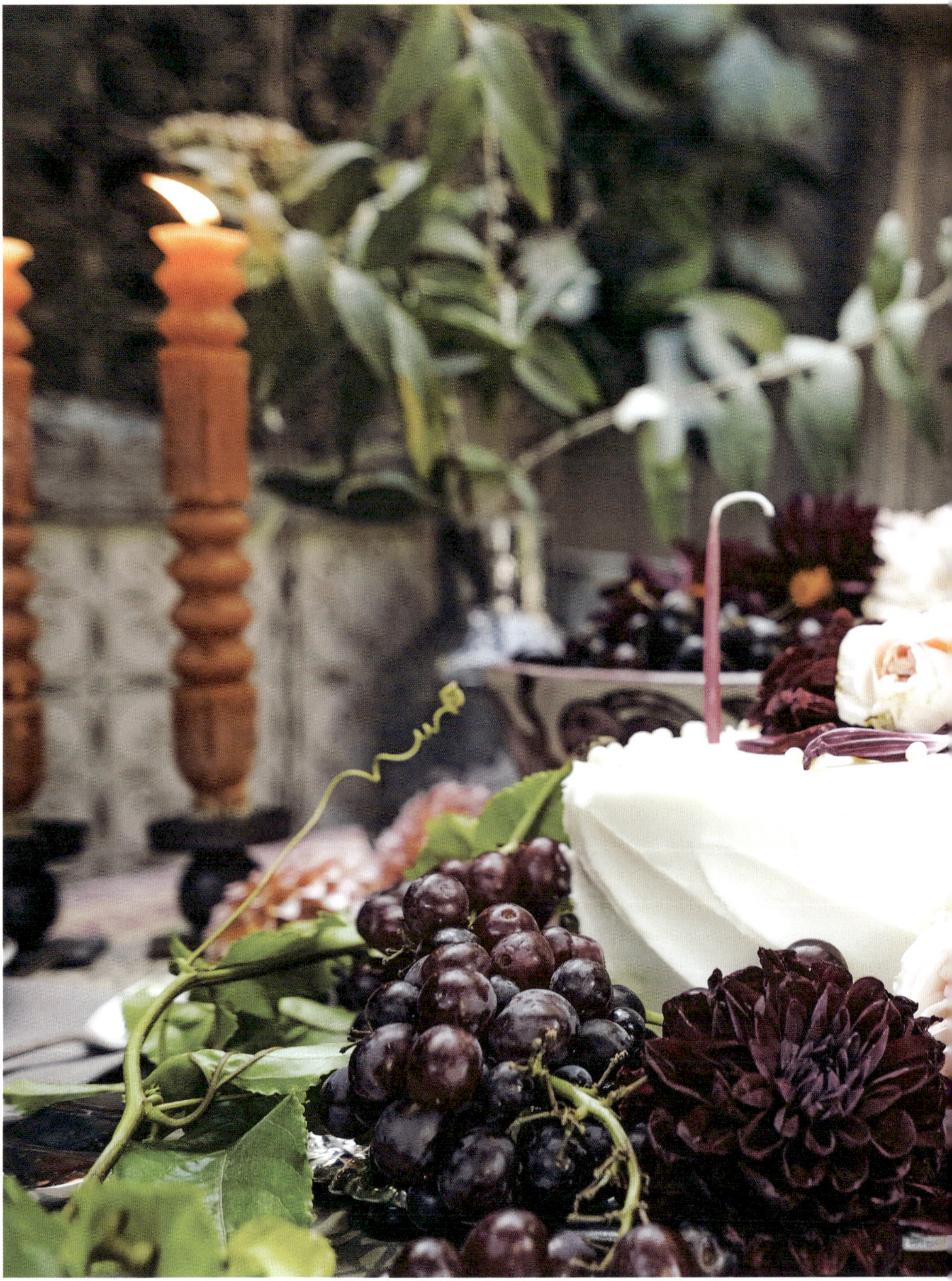

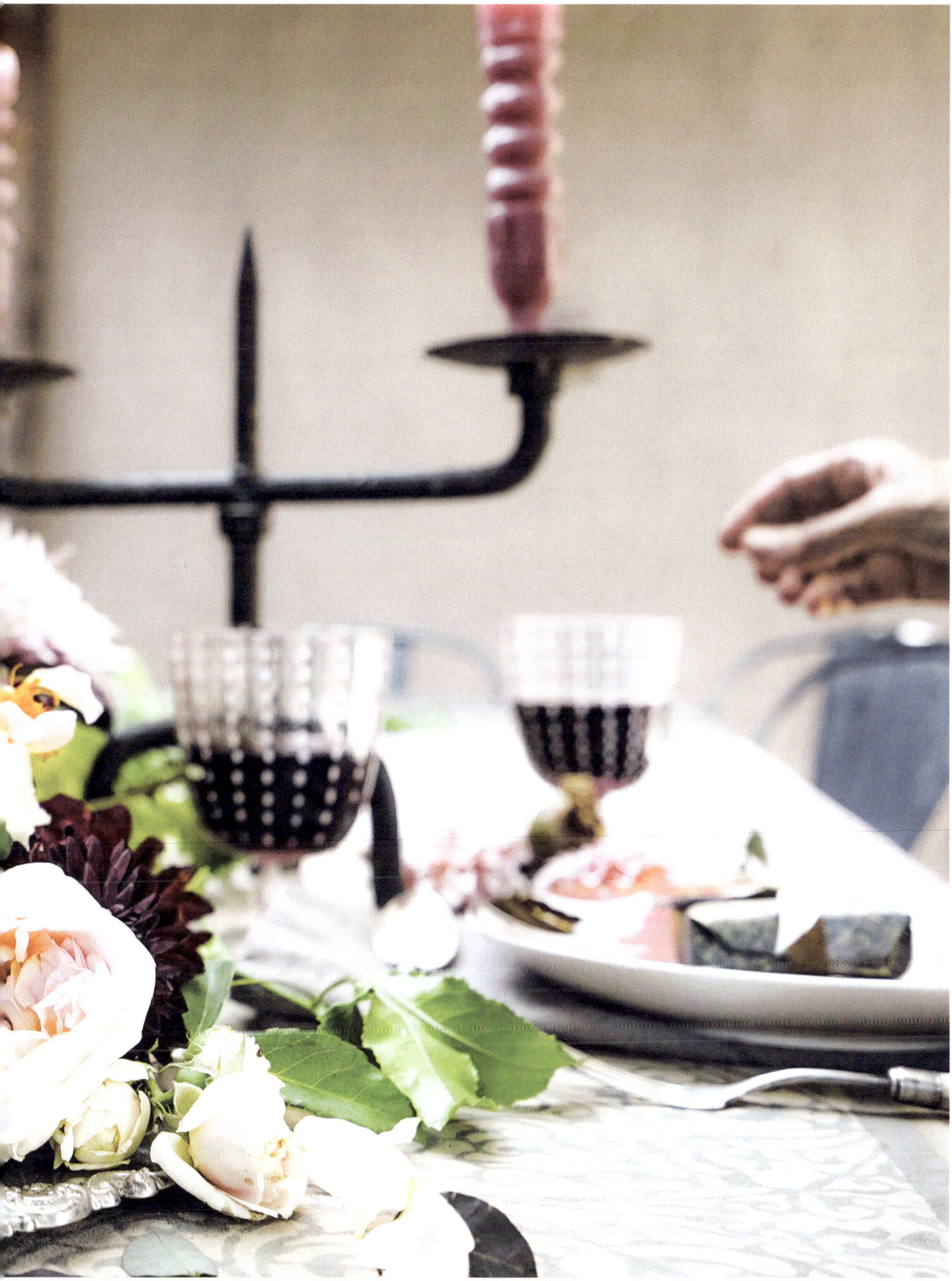

LIFE EVENTS

Saying Goodbye to House and Land

We make most of our memories in our homes and the land they rest on. They hold us through celebration, achievement, joy, sadness, and pain. Our homes are our source of shelter from the world, physically and metaphorically. When a decision is made to leave a home, even for something exciting and new, it comes with an ending—an ending of your relationship with the home and the land it sits on. Acknowledging this separation can help your family (including children and pets) and the spirit of the home to be ready for what is next. This ceremony can be done with just your family members or can include neighbors, relatives, and loved ones who have been an essential part of your memories in the home.

STEPS

» Choose a favorite location in the house for the ceremony. Set an altar with meaningful items and the objects from Nature, light the candle, and burn some blessing herbs or incense. Play soothing music or a favorite playlist.

» Gather the household members close to the altar and invite other participants to form an outer ring surrounding you, with the altar at the center.

» Invite all participants to close their eyes, take a few deep breaths, and become present to the home and land around you.

INTENTION

Thank your home and land for everything you have experienced there so that you can always access the memories wherever you are. Release this home so that you can travel into the world with joy and presence, and so the house can welcome the next occupants freely.

GROUP CEREMONY

TIME NEEDED

45 minutes

ELEMENTS

Mementos from the home, such as soil from the land, pictures, childhood objects, or a piece of holiday decor

(continues on opposite page)

LIFE EVENTS

≫ Invite the four directions (East, South, West, North) into your circle. Invite any ancestors, guides, or spirits to join you in your circle and in ceremony. Invite the spirit of the home and the land you live on to join you.

≫ Breathe deeply to calm your body and begin to feel the energy of the home around you. Invite all participants to see if they can feel the energy or the spirit of the home with their bodies and their hearts. You can say, "Beautiful home that has held us so well, we invite you to connect with us in spirit."

≫ Guide your participants to remember some of the most significant events that occurred in your home. Invite them to hold each memory in their heart for a moment. Someone may remember special holidays or events, planting a garden, bringing a child home for the first time, a graduation, a concert, a special meal, or a cozy rainy day. Guide your participants in a stroll down memory lane, enjoying all the special feelings and times you all have enjoyed in this home. Allow people to say how they feel when they hold these memories. Give everyone time to sit with them, enjoy them, respect them, and experience them.

≫ Invite participants to think of a word or phrase that encapsulates the feeling of this home. They can say it out loud or to themselves. Repeat that phrase or word a few times, infusing it with all the feelings of home. Let participants know that they can use this word or phrase to bring up all the connections and feelings of the home at any time. If you have a special item you have placed on the altar, you can infuse the feeling of the home into this item by holding the item to your heart and sharing your feelings with the object and asking it to hold your memory.

(continues)

Items representing the four elements (preferably from the land): air (feather), water, fire (candle), earth (soil or plant)

Blessing herbs or incense, such as sage, copal, or cedar

Soothing music

Paper and pen

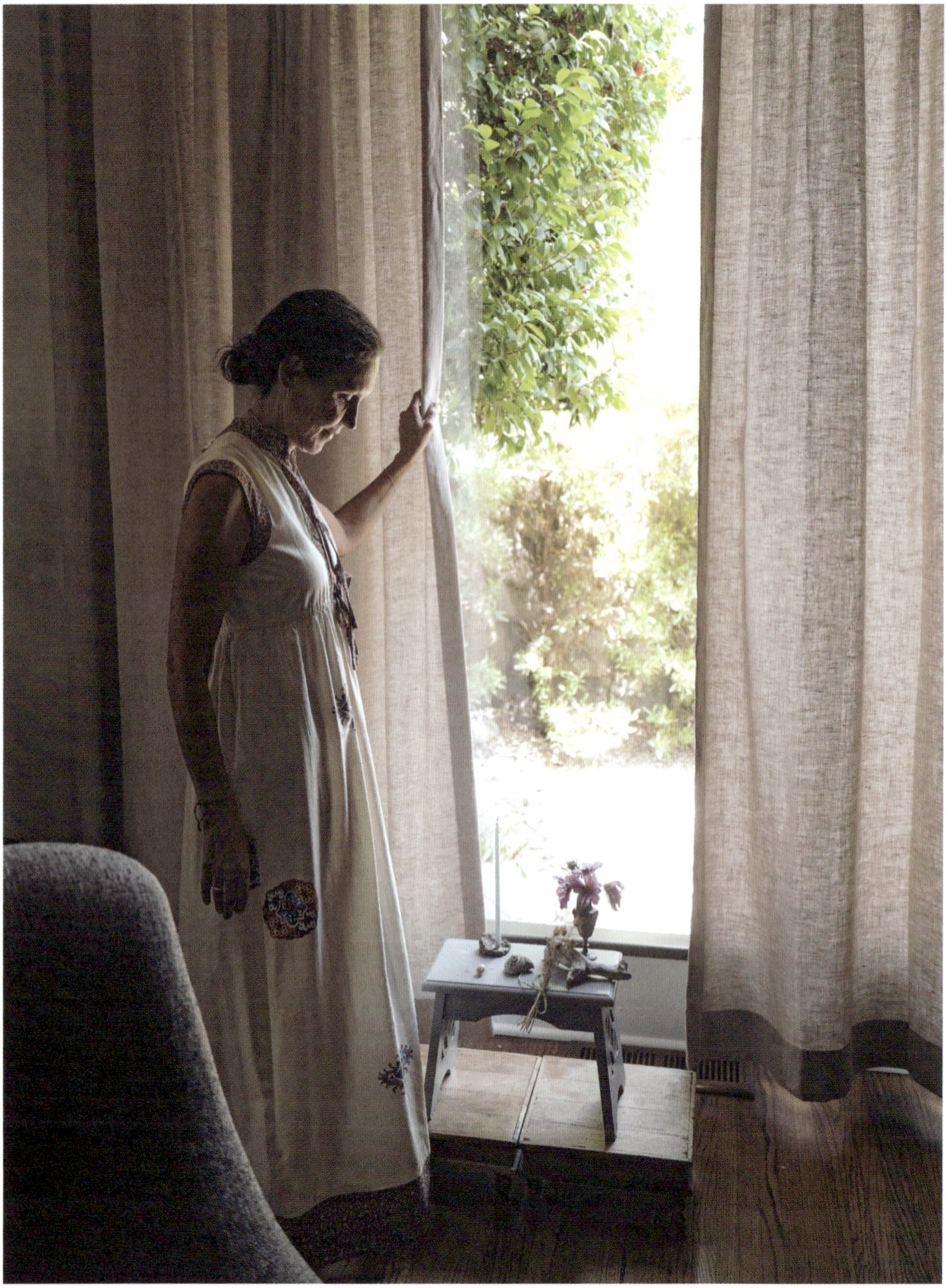

≫ Ask yourself and the participants whether there is anything you want to let go before leaving this home, anything you want to leave behind and not take with you into your next adventure. Thank that thing and let it go. You can blow the thought away to release it into the atmosphere. You can also place the idea of what you are letting go into an item or write it on a piece of paper and burn it to release it, asking the fire to carry your release out to the universe.

≫ Breathe deeply and feel the home and land around you. Thank this home and land with deep gratitude for all it has given you: all the lessons, all the experiences, and all the love. Bless it with devotion. Tell this home and land that you know it will be with you always and that it is welcome to begin to create memories with its new occupants. Release this home, and let it carry your memory, but move on. Maybe leave a blessing for the new inhabitants. You can say, speaking aloud or silently, "Thank you and goodbye, beautiful home. We release you and invite you to form new memories with the next inhabitants."

≫ Thank the four directions and the guides or spirits of the land and house that joined you on your journey for their presence and guidance. Open the circle.

≫ Celebrate with your participants, enjoying food and drink, memories of the home, and excitement for the next phase.

LIFE EVENTS

Blessing a New Home

INTENTION

Introduce yourself to your new home and clear any old energy. Begin a relationship with the new space that will hold you and your family.

GROUP CEREMONY

TIME NEEDED

45 minutes

ELEMENTS

Items from each participant to represent hopes for the new home, such as a favorite book or poem, an ornament to represent holiday gatherings, a dinner plate or napkin for shared meals, or photos of the family and friends you plan to fill your home with

(continues on opposite page)

Moving into a new home is exciting, but with so much to do, it can be overwhelming. This new home will hold you and your family and will quickly fill with love and memories. This ceremony will allow you to start the relationship with your new home in a beautiful way and let the home and land know you are grateful to be there.

STEPS

» Find a space that is quiet and protected. This can be a special place in the home or outside on the land. Set the altar with the objects from you and your family and the items representing the four elements. Light a candle and burn some blessing herbs or incense.

» When you are ready to bless your new home, walk the land in silent devotion. Notice everything. Give blessings to the land; let it know you are so grateful to be there. Honor those who walked and tended the land before you. Say their names if you know them.

» Gather a few items from the land to bring into ceremony with you, such as stones, grasses, moss, or roots. Let the land know you will use the items in ceremony and ask permission to borrow them.

» When you have finished walking the land, move to your ceremony circle. Sit in the sacred space you have created in front of your altar.

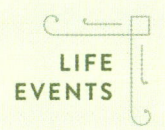

» Ground yourself and others with several deep breaths and become present to the moment and where you are.

» Invite the four directions (East, South, West, North) into your circle. Invite any of your ancestors, guides, or spirits to join you in ceremony. Invite the spirits of the home and the land you live on to join you. You can speak these invitations out loud or silently. See if you can feel the spirits of the land and the home joining you.

» Invite participants to breathe deeply to calm their bodies. Invite them to turn off their minds and instead begin to become aware of their hearts. You can say, "Let your heart become a bright white light and let that light spread over your entire body and out into the space we have created, connecting all of us, including this home and land."

» Now introduce yourselves to your new home and land (and their spirits and ancestors) and let them know you are honored to be in relationship with them. You can each say your names out loud and whisper your wishes and desires to the new home. Let it know you are honored and excited to be there. Bow down if it feels right. Ask the home and land to welcome you.

» Breathe deeply and quietly and see if you can feel anything your new home might want to say to you. Invite your home to speak to you and let it know that you want to honor it. Ask participants to listen with their hearts to feel if the home has any wishes or requests for them. You can say aloud or silently, "Beautiful new home, we are so honored to be living here, and we desire to be in relationship with you. Is there anything you want us to know, or anything you need from us?" Listen. Thank your home for revealing its wishes and needs to you.

(continues)

LIFE EVENTS

Items representing the four elements: air (feather), water, fire (candle), earth (soil or plant)

Incense or blessing herbs, like sage, copal, or cedar

Natural items from the land of your new residence, such as stones, grass, or roots

LIFE EVENTS

≫ When you have accepted the messages from your home, pick up the items from the land, sacred objects, or crystals, and infuse them with your intentions, wishes, and desires for this new home. *Whoosh.* Blow your wishes and prayers into the objects. At the end of the ceremony, place these objects around the home and garden. Perhaps some of these come from your old home. Introduce these items to the new home or land and invite them to be welcomed and remind you of the energy of your old home.

≫ Enjoy a celebration after the ceremony with your family and any invited friends. Perhaps you set out a plate for the spirit of the home and land and feed portions of the food to that plate. When the celebration is over, you can place this plate outside on the land and offer it to the spirits and animals there. If you live in a city, this can be done as a concept of generosity rather than a literal plate outside.

Clearing Stale Energy

If you feel the need to cleanse the new home, light a sage leaf or other blessing herb, such as lavender, copal, cedar, piñon, or an incense stick, and walk from room to room, whispering words of assurance and cleansing. Tell each room you are excited to be there and to create memories together. Tell the home that it is okay to release any old or stale memories or feelings now that you are there. Blow the blessing herb into the corners of the room and invite any stale energy to depart. Open the windows to release any stale energy and to invite fresh, clean energy into the room. Blow love and positivity into each room with the sacred smoke.

On a regular basis, monthly or weekly, close your eyes and feel your new home. How is your relationship? Does it need anything from you? Does it feel comfortable with you and your family? Do you or your family feel anything you want to share with your home or land?

Remember that a relationship takes care and giving. Notice your home and land. How does it change throughout the day and the season? Sing to it, love it, and show it your devotion. What does it sing to you? Even saying a prayer of cleansing and love before cooking a meal can be an act of devotion and love.

LIFE EVENTS

Commitment
VOW RENEWAL

INTENTION
Consciously and intentionally choose your partnership for now and going forward.

YOU AND YOUR PARTNER OR SMALL GROUP IF DESIRED

TIME NEEDED
2 hours

ELEMENTS
Personalized vows written by each partner

Items for an altar, including wedding rings (your current rings), photos of you as a couple and of your loved ones, mementos of your time together, or elements from Nature

Playlist of favorite music

Blessing herbs or incense

Honey, symbolizing sweetness

We make a big deal of weddings in our modern culture, but rarely do we celebrate the ongoing work and commitment it takes to keep a relationship strong. This ceremony is intended to honor the choice we make each day to *stay* married or committed. We are lucky to live in a time when, whether married or in partnership, we have a choice to remain in a relationship. When we consider it this way, a relationship can feel as fresh and vibrant as it did in the beginning.

This ceremony can be performed by the couple alone, or with a group of loved ones gathered as witnesses. You can simply speak your vows to each other, or you can invite a trusted friend to perform the ceremony for you. What is important is to focus on the meaning of the ceremony, the intentional commitment and choice of the couple. You can also make this a beautiful celebration and party, but don't lose the meaning of the recommitment in the details of the party.

STEPS

» Choose an auspicious day for your ceremony. It can be the day you originally married, the anniversary of your first date, or any other day that is special to you. Prepare your new vows or commitments for each other, focusing on the relationship you wish to have going forward and who you both are now.

» Choose a location that is meaningful to you both—a favorite place, the location where you married, even your own backyard. Create a sacred space, with an altar containing photos of yourselves and your loved ones, mementos of your time together, your wedding rings, or items you have given each other. Include flowers or elements of Nature.

» When you are ready to begin, play music that you love, burn some blessing herbs or incense, and enter the sacred space. If you have invited others to join you, you may consider creating a circle of your guests around you, rather than standing at the front with your backs to the group. Follow the next steps in the ceremony yourselves or invite the person you have chosen to conduct the ceremony to lead you through the steps.

» Begin by stating your intention, to consciously choose to commit again to your partner. Invite everything that's meaningful to you to join you in the circle, such as the natural elements, your children and ancestors, the love that brought you together and brought you this far, and your current friendships and faith. If you have others joining you, welcome them and thank them for joining to witness your commitment.

» Breathe deeply and imagine your hearts as bright light, merging the energy from heaven with energy from Earth. Let the light pour out of your hearts and connect you. If you have included others, invite them to let the light from their hearts spill onto you.

» Name some of the best times and best things from your relationship—laugh, cry, give thanks and gratitude for all you have experienced.

» Read out loud the vows that you have prepared. These should be vows that are created for the people you are now—and going into the future. You may reference your original vows but do not be confined by what you pledged in the past.

(continues)

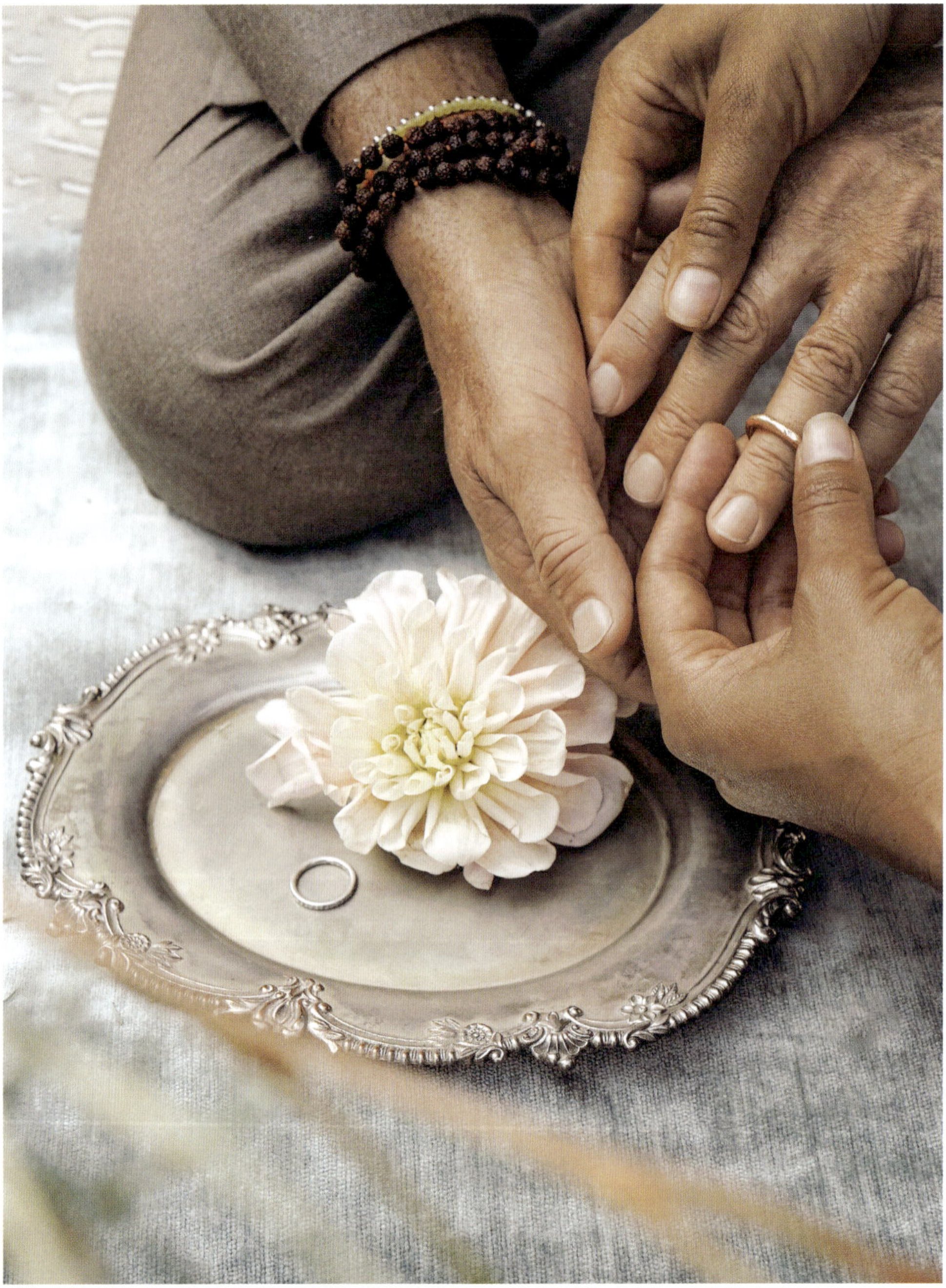

Look at your partner as you read. Listen to your partner with your body, mind, and heart; hear what they are offering and promising to you. When they are finished, say, "I do" or "I gratefully accept your vow."

≫ Take up your rings from the altar, say out loud that you bless the rings, and invite the universe, your ancestors, and your guides to bless the rings. Place the rings on each other, saying, "With this ring, I choose you as my partner, to spend my life with, again, today."

≫ Dip your fingers in the honey and say, "This honey represents sweetness, unity, community, partnership, hard work, and purpose." Taste the honey—on each other's fingers if it feels right. Say, "May this honey remind us to work in partnership and to treat each other with sweetness each day."

≫ Hold hands and say, "We choose each other, we love each other, we are a team," or whatever feels right to you. You can say, "Each day, we will give thanks for the love we share, will treat each other with sweetness and kindness, and will always act in the highest good for the other."

≫ Thank the elements and ancestors for witnessing your vows. If you have invited others to join you, invite them to share their blessing with you. Remind them that you have invited them to witness your vows and that you consider them a key part of your community and your relationship.

≫ Celebrate together with a meal, a swim, or any play activity. Be joyous!

≫ You may choose to repeat this commitment ceremony yearly or at whatever interval feels appropriate to you.

LIFE EVENTS

Divorce
TO MARK THE END OF A RELATIONSHIP

INTENTION

Process the grief and lessons from the ending of a relationship, acknowledge your lessons, and move on.

SOLO CEREMONY

TIME NEEDED

1 hour

ELEMENTS

An object that represents the relationship

Cup or pitcher of water

Candle or fire source

An object that represents strength and hope

Journal/pen

A dessert or sweet treat

What started out in love and excitement and hopes for the future is now coming to an end. Endings can be painful and confusing, but they also offer an opportunity for renewal. A transition has three distinct phases: the ending of something, the messy middle, and the new beginning. This ceremony will help you set the stage to begin your transition and move on in your life by marking the end of the relationship.

Note that this can be the end of a romantic relationship, a friendship, or even a job. Think broadly about how you define a relationship and use this ceremony to work through any kind of ending. You can perform this ceremony alone or with a few trusted witnesses.

STEPS

» If you decide to invite others to witness your ceremony, choose a few trusted people who witnessed the relationship to support you moving on. Prepare them for the ceremony by explaining your intention and their role as witnesses and support for moving on. It may be appropriate to include older children in the ceremony so they can witness your release from the relationship.

» Find a place that is special to you and makes you feel connected to your true self. This can be a park, beach, the woods, or even your backyard. Try to make it a place that is not particularly related to the person you are separating from and somewhere special to *you alone*. Lay out a blanket and

127

set up a small altar with the object from the relationship, a cup or pitcher of water, and a candle.

⟫ Start by taking the object that represents the relationship and its failures. Hold the item, and let all the feelings of failure, sadness, anger, grief, or frustration arise. Concentrate those feelings into the object. Say them out loud and *whoosh* them into the object. You can say, "I hate that they cheated on me," or "My first love is over," and release these feelings into the object. Let it all out. Cry. Scream. Beat your fists on the ground. When you feel empty of the grief and anger, take the object that holds the feelings and burn it or bury it in the ground (if you can do this safely and legally). Ask the fire or the earth to receive your anger and transmute it into hope. If you have guests with you, they can cheer you on and check in with you to make sure that you have truly released everything. This signifies the ending, which becomes the beginning of the transition.

⟫ Next, take the object that represents strength and begin to think through all the lessons you learned in the relationship and all of the good that came from it. Without the grief and anger you have just released getting in the way, try to recall the good times, especially what you have learned. Did you learn to be more patient? To identify and speak your needs? To support yourself? Speak these lessons out loud and into the object that represents hope. Fill the object with your lessons, whisper to it, and treat it with reverence. This object will become your harbinger of hope. It will carry everything forward for you through the messy middle and will be the seed of the new beginning. Pour water on this object to signify cleansing and new beginnings.

⟫ Finally, get your journal and write down five to ten possible new pathways for yourself. Go wild, and don't let reality hem you in. What are the ten wildest things you could do now that you are no longer in the relationship? You could say, "Move to Mexico," or "Change profession," or "Eat dinner at 10 p.m." Let the relationship change signify an ability to be free and think differently about your life. Take the shackles off and think big. You do not have to have a plan for accomplishing any of these things; just write them down. If you have others joining you, you may decide to write these ideas in advance or invite them to contribute wild ideas as well.

» When you are complete, sit for a moment in gratitude. Thank the relationship for its lessons and what it brought you. Breathe deeply and feel the openness in your body replacing anger and grief, filling it with fresh air and sparkling energy. Hold your harbinger of hope in your hands and feel its possibility and power. If you have brought along something sweet, indulge in that now, acknowledging the sweetness of life and all that you have to look forward to. If you have others witnessing your ceremony, thank them for supporting you, and perhaps create a specific request, such as "I would be grateful if you'd check on my progress once a month," or "Please treat me gently as I move through this transition."

LIFE EVENTS

Retirement

TO COMMEMORATE THE
END OF A JOB OR CAREER

INTENTION

Acknowledge the lessons from the job or position you are leaving and generously celebrate those with whom you shared your time. Prepare an open heart and mind for your next adventure.

GROUP CEREMONY

TIME NEEDED

1 hour

ELEMENTS

Pen and small pieces of paper

A bowl or jar

Small, meaningful gifts for your coworkers

A dessert or sweet treat

Most of us spend the majority of our lives working. Whether in a paid position, a volunteer role, or running our own company or household, many of us find meaning in work. Hopefully, the work you do fulfills you, helps you find meaning, and uses your talents.

Thus, when it comes time to leave a job or a profession, whether it be your choice or your employer's choice, you can choose to leave gracefully and with intention. Leaving gracefully will allow you to capture the gifts and benefits of the job and allow you to move on thoughtfully. Rushing through a job ending or burying your feelings about it will not allow you to bring your whole self to your next endeavor, especially if the separation is not your choice. Taking the time to acknowledge the positives will put you in a good position to move on emotionally.

You can hold this ceremony for yourself, or even better, have a friend or coworker help you host this gathering. Do not be afraid to ask for your departure "party" to take on a bit more meaning than just sharing some cake. If it feels more comfortable, you can hold this celebration at home or outside of your workplace.

STEPS

» Invite your coworkers and family members to celebrate the conclusion of your time at this job. You can let them know that you will be acknowledging what you did while at the position or what you have accomplished together. Indicate that this will be a meaning-making ceremony, so they are prepared.

» When all guests have gathered, you can speak. If you feel uncomfortable, invite a friend to give you prompts to answer so it's more of a dialogue. Speak about these topics:

- *What did you learn from this position that you will be carrying with you into the future?*
- *What are you leaving behind or releasing?*
- *What were the best things you accomplished in the position, or what are you proud of?*
- *How did you feel when you first started the position, and how do you feel now?*
- *Tell a funny story from work.*
- *Which coworkers did you learn from?*

» You can invite (or have a friend invite) your coworkers to think about a favorite memory, one of their favorite things about you, or what they will miss when you leave. Then, have them write that thought on a small piece of paper and place it in a bowl or jar. Read these sentiments later when you are alone and savor all that transpired in the position.

» If you have brought gifts for anyone, give them out with sincere thanks and an open heart.

» When you have finished reflecting, celebrate with something sweet, symbolizing the sweetness of your experience in the position. Or invite a friend to create a special cocktail or mocktail to toast with. Thank your coworkers and family for joining you and thank the position for what it gave you.

(continues)

Good luck in
your next adventure
please stay in touch
with all of us. J.
TOPHER BOYER

≫ Later, write down some of your thoughts and feelings about your position. You can answer these prompts:

- *Summarize the position and your time there: What happened? How do you feel about it? What were the key lessons? What do you want to avoid repeating? What are you letting go of?*

- *Think about where you are now: How do you feel about leaving? What does the in-between feel like? What are you hoping to bring in for the next phase, either retirement or a new job? How do you feel more prepared or different?*

- *Begin to consider what's next. What do you feel called to? What feels exciting? What have you been ignoring that you now have time for? What is a definite "NO" for you?*

≫ You do not have to rush into anything. Make sure you take the time to properly process the transition to a new job or retirement by gathering the lessons of the past and reflecting on all that is available to you now.

LIFE EVENTS

Dealing with Illness

Receiving a diagnosis of a serious illness is like a dividing point in your life, whether it is your own diagnosis or that of someone you love. There is the before, and there is the after. One day, you are living your life, worrying about what to make for dinner, and the next, you are overcome with fear, anxiety, worry, and usually lots of appointments. In the midst of the flurry of activity, it can be very helpful to mark the moment for yourself and those around you. Take some time to acknowledge that the anger, fear, grief, and possibly hopefulness provide a way to have a little bit of control over your situation.

You can do this ceremony alone or with a few of your closest loved ones, with or without the person who is ill. It can be a good way for children to express their feelings about a diagnosis and learn to move through the stages of grief. Be sure to create enough time for this ceremony and a quiet space to rest in afterward, as you may feel emotionally spent.

STEPS

» If you will include others in the ceremony, reach out to invite them, sharing your intention. Think about inviting those who will support you through the illness and have the strength and capacity to be there for you.

» On the day of your ceremony, find a quiet and meaningful place to gather. State your intention, acknowledging that you did not ask for this diagnosis but are willing to accept it and process it.

(continues)

INTENTION

Make meaning from the changes about to happen in your life and move through the emotions from fear to hope.

SOLO OR SMALL GROUP CEREMONY

TIME NEEDED

45 minutes

ELEMENTS

3 candles in different colors, to represent the emotions you are experiencing

Journal/pen

134

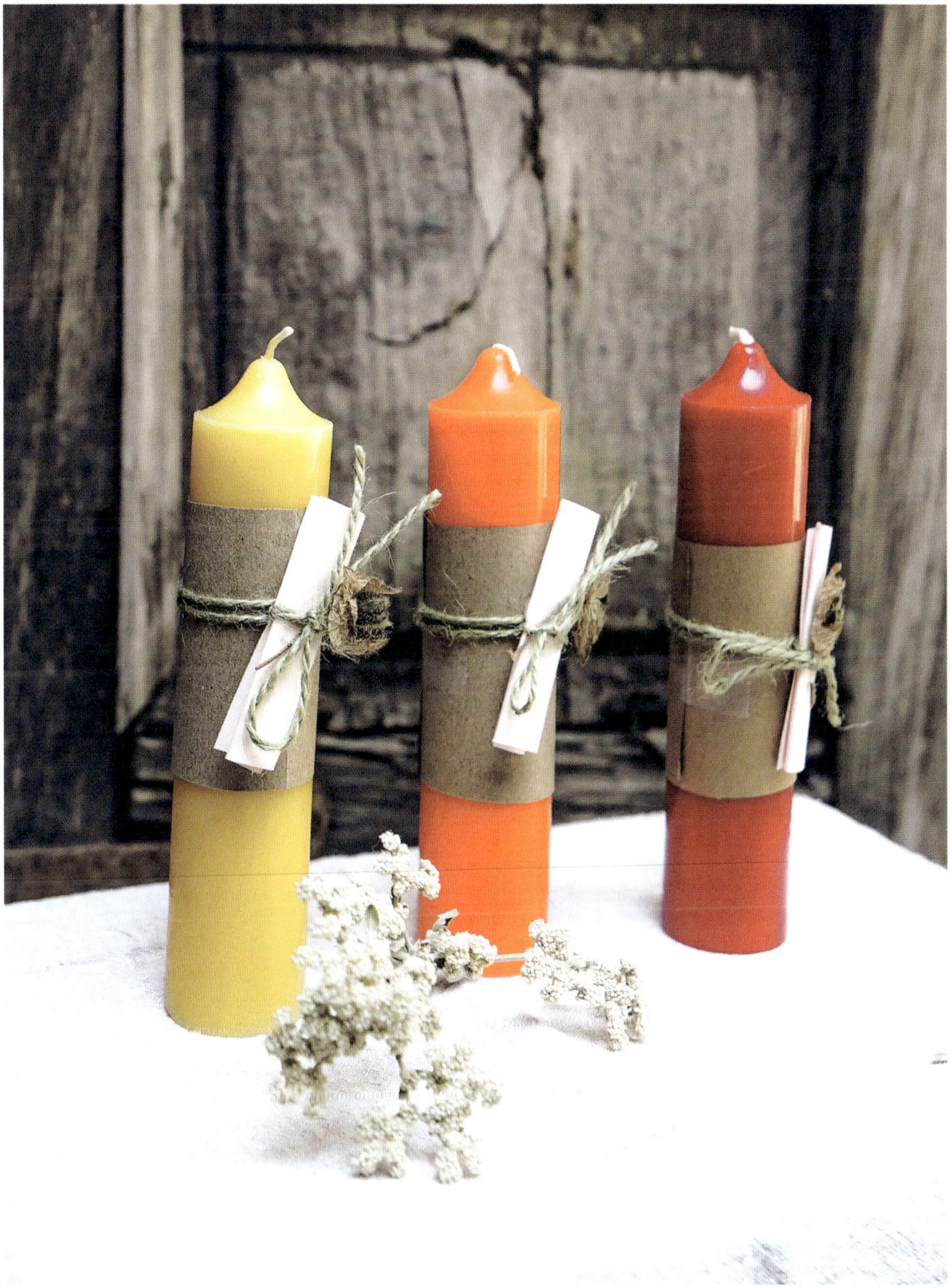

LIFE EVENTS

≫ Light the first candle, preferably red, which symbolizes anger. Anger is the first step in this grieving process. Once you have lit the candle, use words and actions to express your anger at receiving the diagnosis—for yourself or a loved one. Let it all out. Scream. Pound the floor, break something. Rage. Invite the others to rage with you. When you feel complete, blow out the candle and say, "I acknowledge the anger and rage that I am feeling due to this diagnosis."

≫ Light the second candle for grief. Now let all of your feelings of grief arise: fear, depression, anxiety, worry, sadness, uncertainty. Name your deepest fears out loud. Cry. Fall apart. Worry about what you are losing, what will never be the same again. Invite your loved ones to express their fears as well. This may be difficult, so just experience and sit with whatever comes up. When you are complete, say, "I acknowledge the fear and grief that I am feeling from this diagnosis. Thank you for letting me release."

≫ Light the third candle, ideally in an uplifting color, such as yellow, purple, green, or pink, for hope. As you light this candle, begin to think about the positive things you have in your life: the love around you, the treatments you or your person are eligible to receive, what *hasn't* gone wrong in the diagnosis, what you are grateful for, and what you hope for. You can say, "I am so grateful that we are aware of this illness and that we have the best doctors to help." And "I am loved, and though I am nervous about the future, this illness will teach me to cherish every day." Let your hope and gratitude flow over. Acknowledge the big and the small things.

≫ When you feel complete, let your candle continue to burn while you hold hands with those in your circle if they are present. Feel the love that connects you even if you are alone in ceremony. Send your deepest love and prayers to the person with the diagnosis (especially if that is you) and let them know that you will always hold them in your circle of love and strength. It can also be very helpful to write in a journal the feelings that you have felt at each step throughout the ceremony.

》 If you find this ceremony helpful, commit to gathering in a circle frequently, even from a distance, to hold your loved one close in your thoughts and send them strength or to care for yourself. You could agree to keep them in your thoughts every morning upon waking or agree to gather once a month to check in and clear out anger and fear before moving on to hope. Acknowledge that you may feel all of the emotions over and over. That is okay; the intention is to keep moving toward hope.

LIFE EVENTS

Menopause: Becoming a Wise Woman

INTENTION
Leave behind the intensity of the "Mother Phase" and welcome the gifts of "Wise Woman" phase. Reclaim your own creativity and energy for yourself.

GROUP CEREMONY

TIME NEEDED
1 hour

ELEMENTS
Mementos from the Motherhood phase

Candle for each participant

Large bowl of water

Journal or paper/pen

Object that feels inspirational, such as a ring, a special crystal, or a piece of clothing

Foods that represent reward and abundance

With each life season, there is a rite of passage or initiation that marks the end of one season and the beginning of the next. It is a time of transformation; the woman transforms from one way of being to another, never to return to her previous life season. What happens during and around this transition, whether by conscious creation or by default, sets the theme for a woman's experience of herself in her new role in her next life season.

—JANE HARDWICKE COLLINGS,
"The Four Phase Feminine Way"

The four phases of a woman's life are maidenhood, motherhood, wise woman, and crone. For some women, moving from the Mother phase (whether or not you physically gave birth) into the Wise Woman phase is marked by going through menopause, which can be painful (hello, hot flashes), disorienting (brain fog), and depressing (feeling invisible). There are many positives of menopause, when a woman stops pouring out energy and blood to others, often to the point of depletion, and instead contains her energy internally because she is no longer shedding a uterine lining. Her womb space, a source of creation and creativity, becomes hers again. During this time, it is essential for a woman to reconnect to the energy of the womb and reclaim time and focus for her own projects.

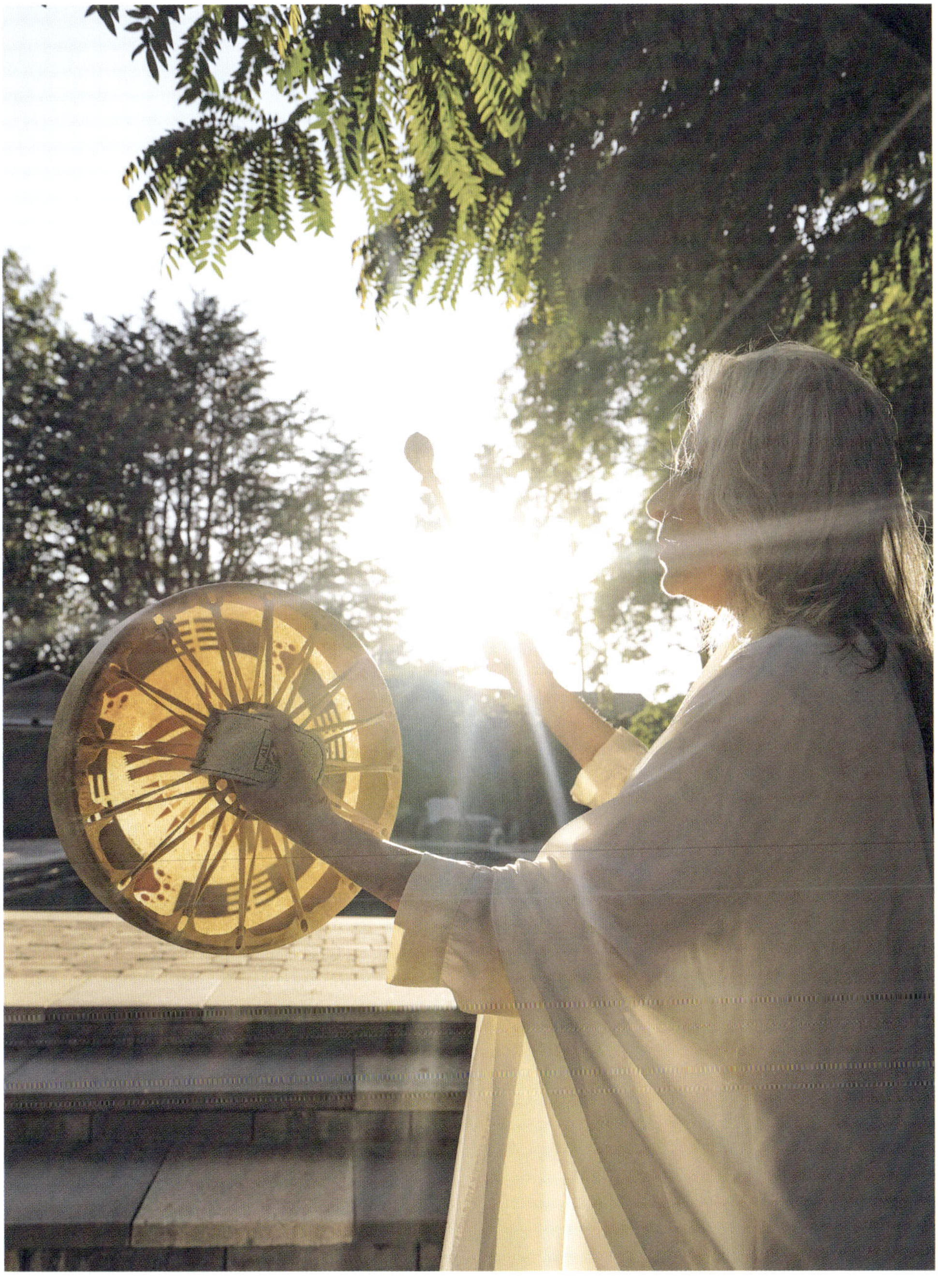

LIFE EVENTS

She is able to harvest the wisdom of her life and focus on the abundant creativity of the womb space, which is represented by water, the life-giving force.

In this ceremony, women are invited to consider their lives in the larger world, carefully protect their boundaries, say "no" to things that do not serve them, and get in touch with what really matters to them. You are invited to make this ceremony a true celebration of this new phase and what is to come after, thanking your body for all the work it has done to create life and abundance for others. Gather your most trusted friends and celebrate yourselves together, or gather your family and invite them to witness you as you move on from spending much of your time caring for them to focusing on your own plans and desires.

STEPS

≫ Set up your ceremony space in a beautiful and special location that honors the life journey you and your beloveds have been on. You can create an altar that holds mementos from your journey through your Mother phase, whether or not you are a mother.

≫ Invite your group to gather in the space. Each participant should place their item on the altar and then sit in a circle facing each other.

≫ Begin by inviting the spirits of all women and ancestors to join you. You can invite your specific ancestors and include the spirit of the great Mother Earth. Invite abundance, care, nurturing, and maternal energy into your circle. Feel this energy; invite your group to feel the benevolence and love surrounding them.

≫ Invite each participant to meditate on the joys of motherhood or the Mother phase. How have each of you been able to nurture others and care for the world? You could go around the circle and allow each participant to name one thing about the Mother phase they are thankful for. If your family is with you, invite them to say out loud how you have cared for them and the gifts you have provided them.

» Next, have each woman light a candle. This candle represents the Mother phase. Gaze into the flame and notice how it burns and flickers. Acknowledge the energy that the flame represents and how it has fueled you through Mother phase. Thank the flame, and let it know, and yourself know, you are ready to move on to another exciting phase.

» When you are ready, blow out the flame.

» Now, pass the bowl of water around the circle and invite each participant to dip her hands into the water and sprinkle it on her body. As the water lands, feel the powerful force of creation enter your body. Invite participants to feel the water connect to the water in their womb space (this may be a symbolic space). Feel the womb space activate and power up, free from the energy needed to build up menstrual blood each month, and then shed it. You can say, "We invite the water in this vessel to activate the creative waters of our womb spaces."

» Invite each participant to consider what projects or ideas are coming up. What feels like it wants to germinate and blossom? What have you been putting off because you are too busy? Feel the energy of these ideas grow inside you.

(continues)

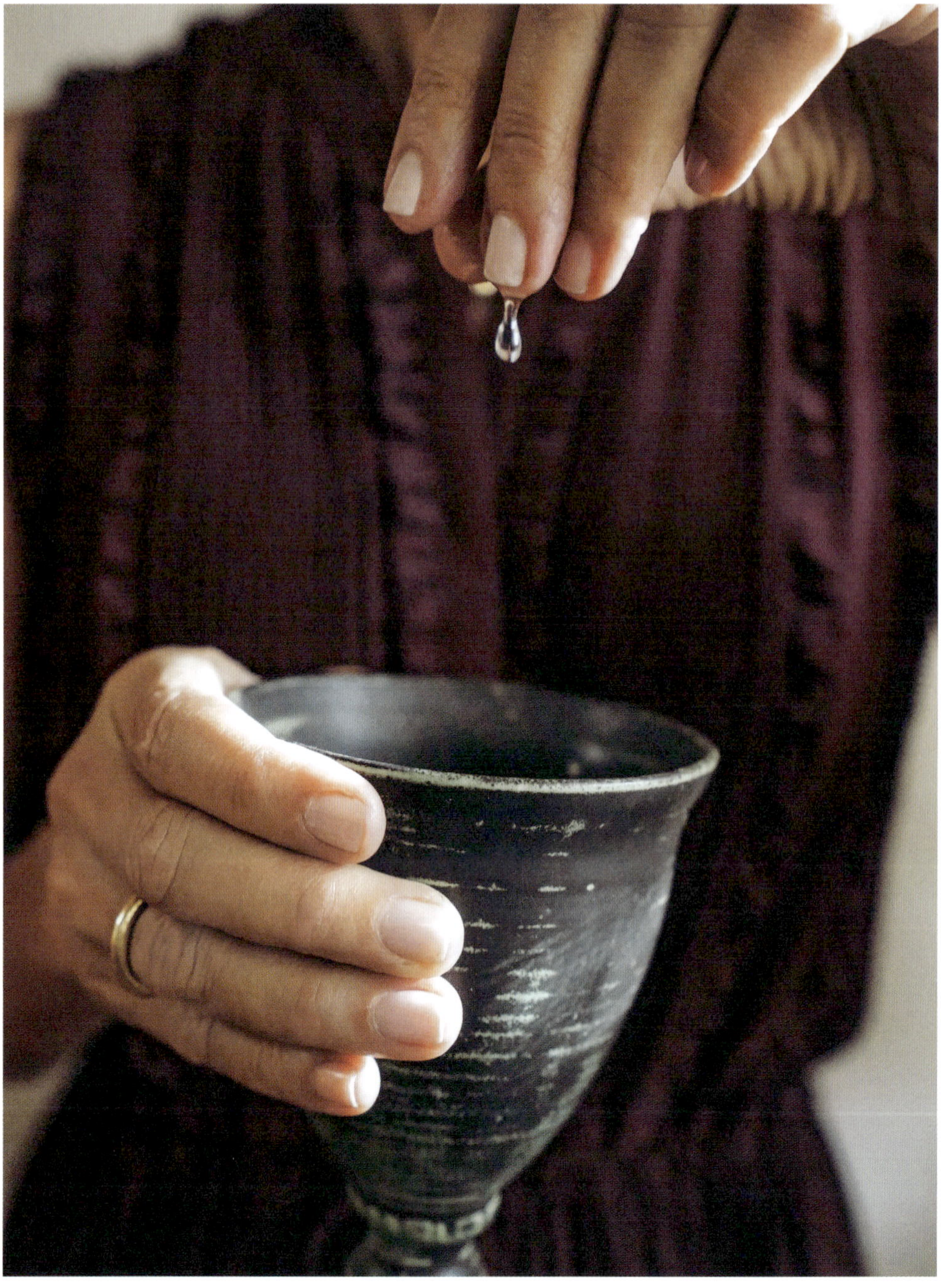

≫ Now consider what you want to say "no" to. Don't use your brain; use your heart and body, and feel the "yes" or "no" arise as you think through things you may want to do or not want to do. Give yourself permission to say "no" to anything that does not feel like an absolute "YES!"

≫ When you feel complete, write down the projects or ideas that feel like a "YES" and the activities that definitely feel like "No" in your journal.

≫ Take the object of importance that you brought and focus your "YES" idea onto the object. Let it carry all the opportunity and abundance you have dreamed of. Each time you look at, hold, or wear this object, the potent energy of these ideas will surround you.

≫ Now would be a good time to share around your circle. Let each participant share one thing they are feeling excited about and one boundary or "no" they are clear about.

≫ When you feel complete, thank the feminine energies you invited to join you in a circle and release them. Let your participants know that together, you hold and represent tremendous energy. They can tap into that energy anytime by simply placing their hands over their womb space or looking at their object.

≫ Follow the ceremony with a feast of foods that represent sweetness and abundance. Celebrate your wisdom and all you have created and accomplished during the Mother phase. Celebrate moving on and the potentiality of the Wise Woman phase. You are a Wise Woman now!

LIFE EVENTS

Living Funeral
CELEBRATION OF LIFE

INTENTION

Celebrate the life of a loved one along with them.

GROUP CEREMONY

TIME NEEDED

1 hour

ELEMENTS

Photos of the honoree and their loved ones

Music

Favorite foods

Items from Nature, including flowers

Letters, poems

Mementos from the honoree's life

In most cultures, the life of a loved one is celebrated after the person has passed away. This ceremony gives a twist on the traditional funeral. It celebrates life while the person is still alive, allowing the person to enjoy the love and appreciation normally expressed in a funeral so they can carry it with them on their way to the afterlife. It is a tremendous gift to offer this celebration to someone at the end of their life, and an honor to get to participate in bringing your presence and devotion to someone you love.

It is not always possible to know when a person will pass, so the timing of this ceremony can be difficult to gauge. Often, by the time we are willing to acknowledge that someone will pass, they can be beyond cognizance. So the advice is to celebrate early, while the loved one can appreciate and receive the love. Think of it as a preparation for a departure and a great journey. Fuel your loved one with memories, wishes, and appreciation as they prepare to move on to the next phase. This is truly a celebration of *life*, not death.

STEPS

» Determine the best time to celebrate a life before someone has passed, but while they are still aware and strong enough to receive your thoughts. It is important to clear the idea of a ceremony with the person being celebrated to make sure they are up for it. If a group gathering together is too much, you may want to have attendees visit in smaller groups. You could also have a ceremony with a small group and record it for others to watch later.

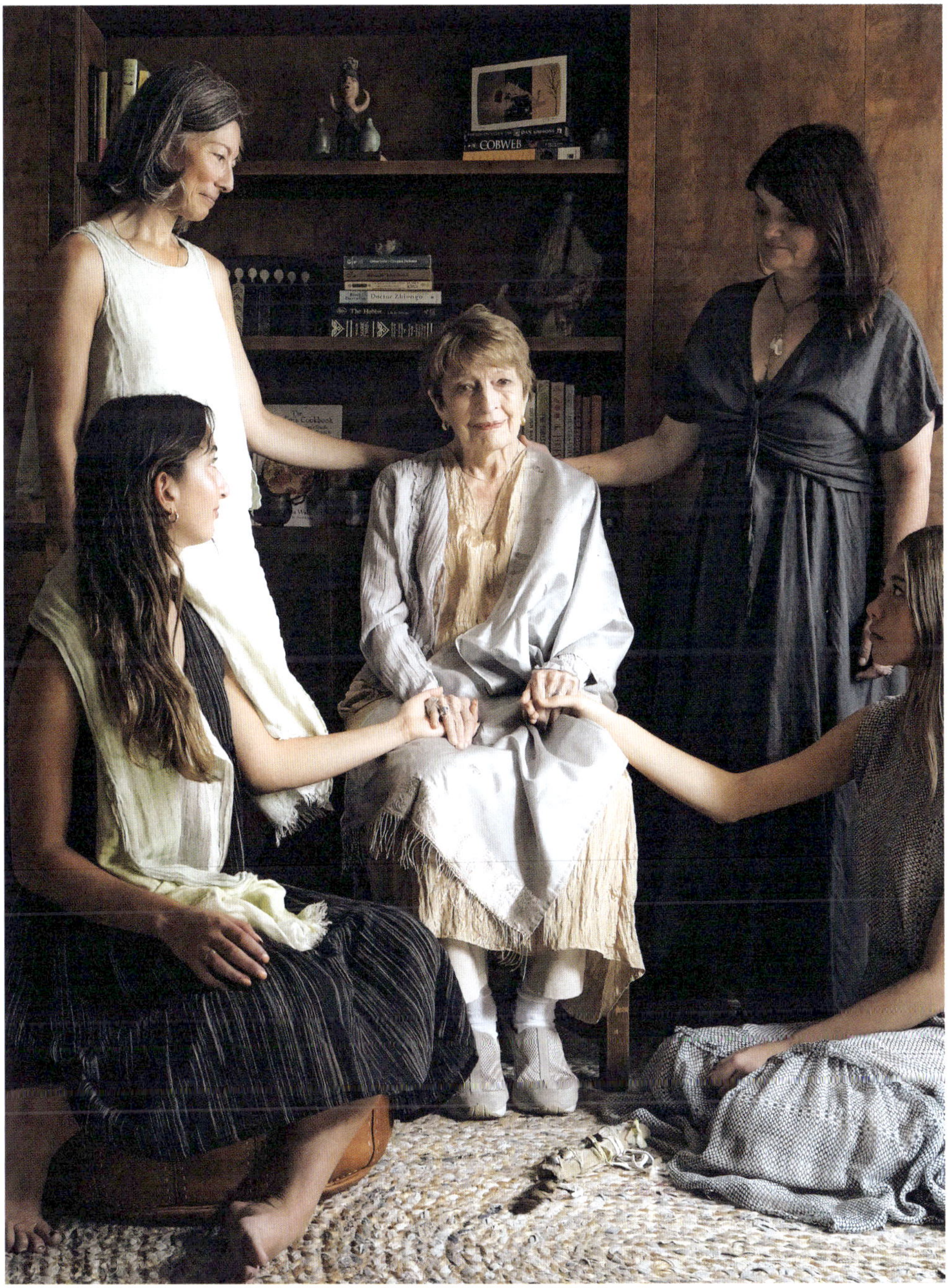
COBWEB
Doctor Zhivago
The Hobbit

LIFE EVENTS

» Invite those most loved by the person being celebrated to attend, reminding them of the honor and the opportunity that spending their last moments with their loved one represents. Invite them to come prepared to share a story, memory, or favorite thing about the celebrant. They can bring photos to share, music, favorite food, items from Nature, letters, and poems. This would be similar to a traditional funeral but will also allow the celebrant to participate.

» On the day of the celebration, make the room festive with flowers and items from Nature, decorations, mementos, and favorite foods, just as you would for any other celebration or party. Gather the group in a circle around the celebrant.

» Begin the ceremony by stating your intention. You can say, "We are gathered to celebrate the incredible life of our father [grandfather, uncle, husband, friend]. We are honored to be able to spend this time celebrating his life while he is still with us."

» Now speak directly to the celebrant with a tribute and some facts about them. For example, you could say, "Dad, I love what a wonderful teacher you are, that you love fishing and watching sappy movies, and you always prepared the most amazing Thanksgiving dinner." In this overview, share facts, saving the memories for the participants to share.

» Next, invite each guest to share a memory, story, photo, or tribute to the celebrant. Do not be afraid to hold the hand or stroke the head of the celebrant. Let them know they are loved and cherished. If words do not come easily, you can guide the discussion with prompts such as "Dad is such a great woodworker. I love the bird feeder he made for the front porch" or "Mom is the best baker. My favorite dish is her _____." Another prompt can be to acknowledge

LIFE EVENTS

the body, such as "Dad had the best hair; it was always flowing in the wind."

» Continue to contribute love and stories until you feel complete. The celebrant can also offer appreciation or final words of wisdom if this is available, which can provide incredible closure that is often not available in death.

» After the celebrant passes, you may not feel a need to have a traditional funeral, as you may feel connected and complete with your memories. For those who were not present at your ceremony, you can consider sharing the recording.

CEREMONIES FOR PERSONAL GROWTH

To connect with
your inner wisdom

While the prior chapter, Ceremonies for Life Events, was about external events, this chapter explores ceremonies that you create for your personal growth: to call in a feeling or energy (such as strength and protection) or to stoke or celebrate parts of your life. When we consciously nurture strong relationships—with ourselves, friends, or Mother Earth—we can feel more grounded and connected to the healing wisdom within us all.

Some of the ceremonies initiate personal growth by commemorating external parts of our lives, like Honoring Land and Mother Earth (page 173). This ceremony is a beautiful practice for developing a reverent relationship with the land around you. Others, like Connecting to the Wisdom of the Heart (page 158), invite you to quiet your conscious mind and attune to the insight of your heart, a beautiful ceremony to practice regularly.

The ceremonies in this chapter can be as big or as small as you like and performed as often as you like. A ceremony that is repeated daily becomes a nourishing, personal ritual, and performing it over and over can impart meaning and bring new lessons each time you perform it.

CEREMONIES FOR

Cleansing and Renewal
152

Protection and Strength
155

Connecting to the Wisdom of the Heart
158

Changing Mindset
162

Integration
165

Celebrating Friendship
169

Honoring Land and Mother Earth
173

PERSONAL GROWTH

Cleansing and Renewal

INTENTION
Remove negative energy and create space for new beginnings.

SOLO CEREMONY

TIME NEEDED
15 minutes

ELEMENTS
Sacred smoke or blessing herbs

Chakapa (bunch of dried palm fronds tied together)

This ceremony can be used anytime you feel a need for cleansing or renewal, such as after an intense experience, at the end of the year, or in preparation for a journey. With these steps, you can create a full-blown ceremony or a shortened version for daily use.

This ceremony calls for using a chakapa (*sha-ka-pah*), a bunch of dried palm fronds used ceremonially in Peru, Equador, and Columbia. The chakapa is used to shake the negative energy out of a body or object and is also used rhythmically to create sacred sound. You can make your own chakapa from palm fronds or other dried plant fronds tied together or find one for purchase (see Resources, page 184). If you make your own chakapa, be sure to focus your attention as you create it with loving, healing energy.

STEPS

» Create a sacred space to perform your ceremony. You can choose a location inside—or, even better, outside, near a body of water, under a tree, or on a mountaintop. Light some blessing herbs to sanctify the space.

» Call in the directions. Invite the fresh energy of the East to join you in your ceremony, representing new beginnings. Invite the fire energy of the South to be present to help burn away any negativity. Invite the watery energy of the West to bring creativity, and invite the grounded energy of the North to ground you. Invite the energies of above, below, and

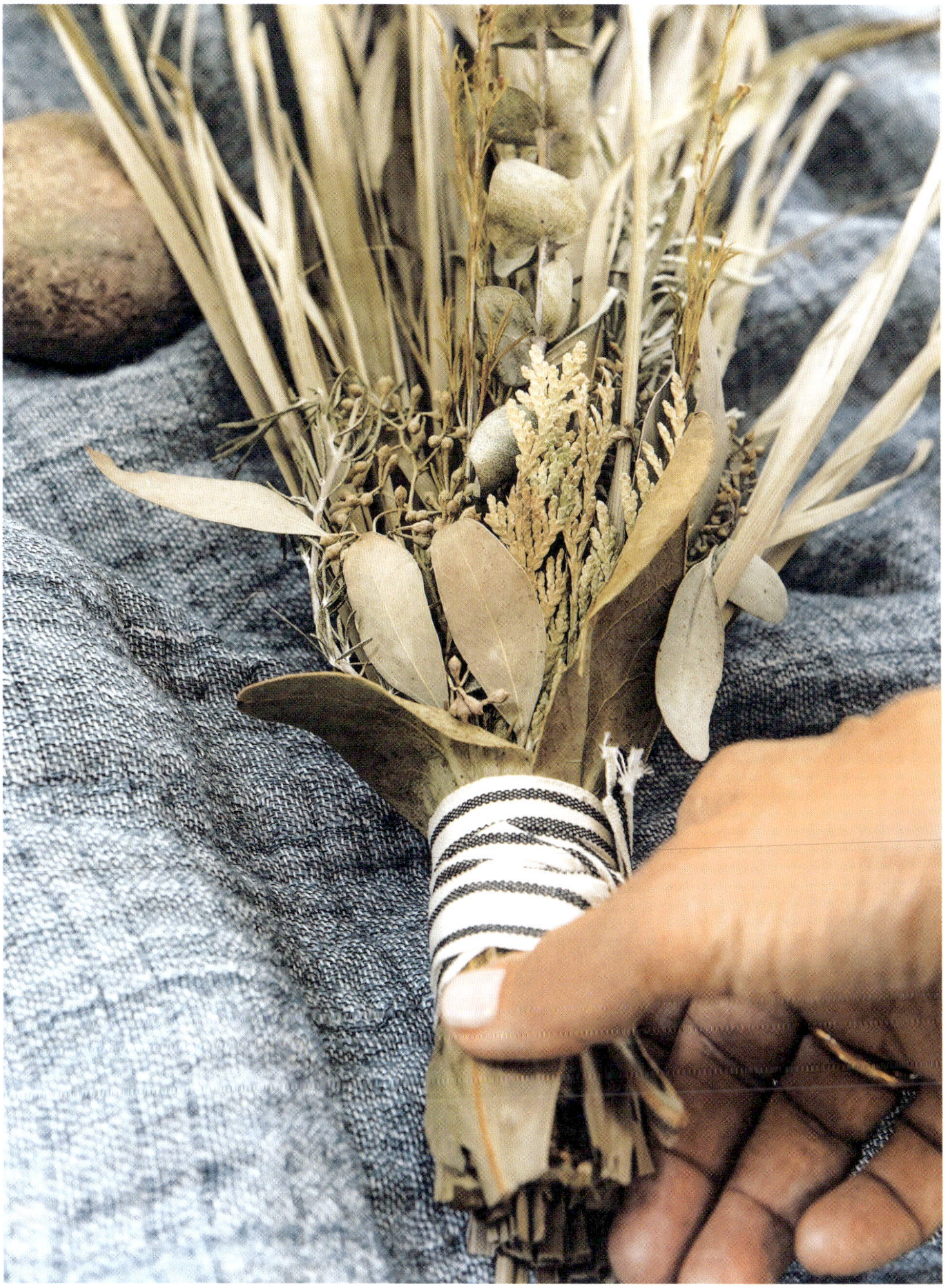

PERSONAL GROWTH

within. Breathe deeply to feel the energies of the directions all around you.

» State your intention for cleansing. For example, you can say, "I am here to cleanse myself from the negativity of the past three months," or "I wish to release my old views about _____ and start fresh."

» To perform the cleansing, shake the chakapa around your body, starting at your head and moving over your entire body, down to your feet. Keep doing this until you feel clear. Once the shaking is complete, release the energy from the chakapa by blowing on it or tapping it on the ground. You can say, "I have gathered all the negative [or stale, or old] energy, and now I release this energy so I can feel cleansed and start fresh."

» Thank the directions for joining you and participating in your cleansing. Breathe deeply and feel how easily energy moves through your body now that you are cleansed. Take three big inhales and exhales.

Cleansing another person

To perform this ceremony for another person, follow the same steps but invite them to share their intention of what they want to cleanse. As you shake the chakapa over them, you can say, "We are cleansing [person's name] so that they may be clear to [repeat their intention]." When you are complete, you can invite them to share how they feel or what they will replace the cleansed energy with.

PERSONAL GROWTH

Protection and Strength

The world is full of information and stimulation, and not all of us can function well in the onslaught. If you are a sensitive person, it's important to protect yourself so that you do not take on too much of the pain and emotions around you. You can think of this as strengthening your auric field—the field of energy that extends out beyond your body.

This ceremony can be practiced when you feel your energy reserves and boundaries getting low or daily for fortification.

STEPS

» Find a quiet spot to sit that feels calm and has positive energy. Light your candle and blessing herbs, and play calming music.

» Breathe deeply and tune in to your body. Feel your body connected to the Earth. Begin to empty any negative or stagnant energy into the Earth. Breathe in and down, and move all stagnant energies down, down, down, through your body, through the floor, down into the Earth. Breathe deeply and blow out. You can also shake your body. Move your body in any way that feels like it will release energy. Do this until your body feels empty and clear. If it feels right to you, you can thank the Earth for accepting your unwanted energy and ask her to compost it.

INTENTION
Create an auric field of protection around yourself so you can function in the world without becoming depleted.

SOLO CEREMONY

TIME NEEDED
15 minutes

ELEMENTS
Candle
Blessing herbs
Calming music

(continues)

155

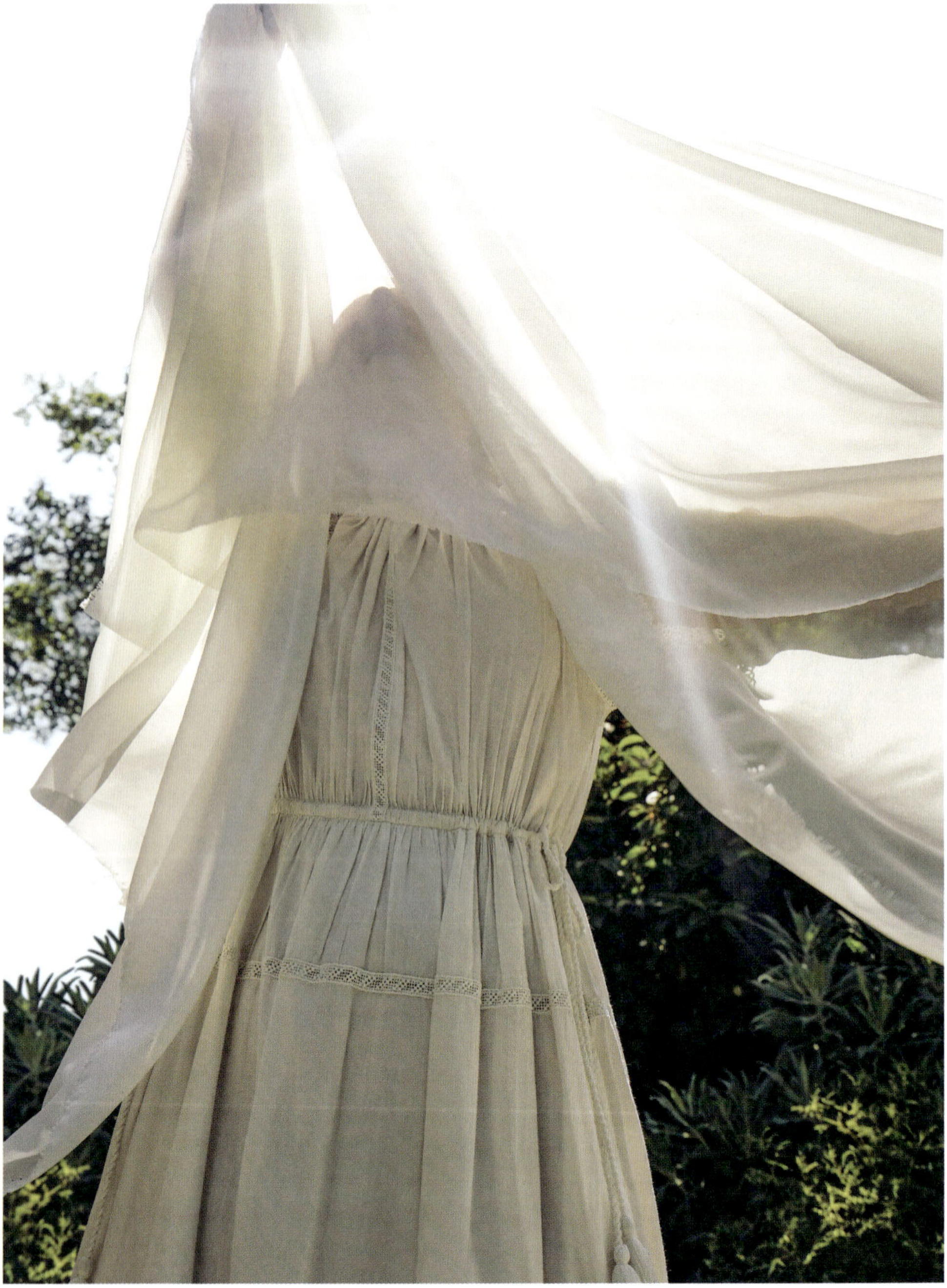

» Take a few cleansing breaths with deep inhales. Allow the fresh, clean air to cleanse your body.

» Now close your eyes and imagine a bubble of light emanating from your body, out in all directions. You might imagine this to be a bright white or golden light, or it may take on another color, like pink, violet, or blue. Concentrate on this bubble of light extending from your body out in all directions, up to 4 feet. Feel it shimmering around you.

» Now call in assistance to make this surrounding light a strong protector for you. You can say, "I call in the light, my angels, my ancestors, and my guides to create protection around me." If you feel a connection to a particular deity, element, or animal, call that in. Whatever you associate with strength and protection, verbally call it in and ask for its help to protect you and contribute to your auric field.

» When you feel complete, open your eyes and feel your field of protection around you. If you find that you need it during the day, close your eyes and imagine the field again, sensing that it is there around you, protecting you and giving you energy and strength.

PERSONAL GROWTH

Connecting to the Wisdom of the Heart

INTENTION

Quiet the mind and tune in to the messages and wisdom of your heart.

SOLO CEREMONY

TIME NEEDED

15 minutes

ELEMENTS

Calming, atmospheric music

Candles

Journal or paper/pen

We spend most of our time in our heads—thinking, analyzing, planning, processing. Our minds are essential for work and keeping our lives on track, but they do not provide the whole picture. Our hearts actually contain far more intelligence than our minds. (Learn more at heartmath.org.)

This is a very simple ceremony for connecting to your heart and tuning in to its intelligence.

STEPS

» Start by getting very comfortable. You can sit or lie down as you wish. Breathe deeply and ground your body. Feel the Earth supporting you. Play calming music, and light candles if you wish.

» Begin by letting your mind know that you are going to give it a rest. Just say, "Thank you, mind. I invite you to relax for a while and to be quiet." Breathe deeply and unfocus.

» Place your hand on your heart. Breathe in and feel your heart. Focus on your heart. Speak to your heart, silently. Ask your heart to speak to you. Say, in your own words, "Beautiful heart, I am listening to you. Tell me what you are feeling or desiring." Keep listening and know that the heart does not always speak in words. The heart often speaks in feelings or in ways we cannot understand with our rational minds. Just trust that your heart will speak to you if you listen and stay quiet. Stay with your heart for a while. You can continue to ask your heart questions, such as "Heart, what do I need

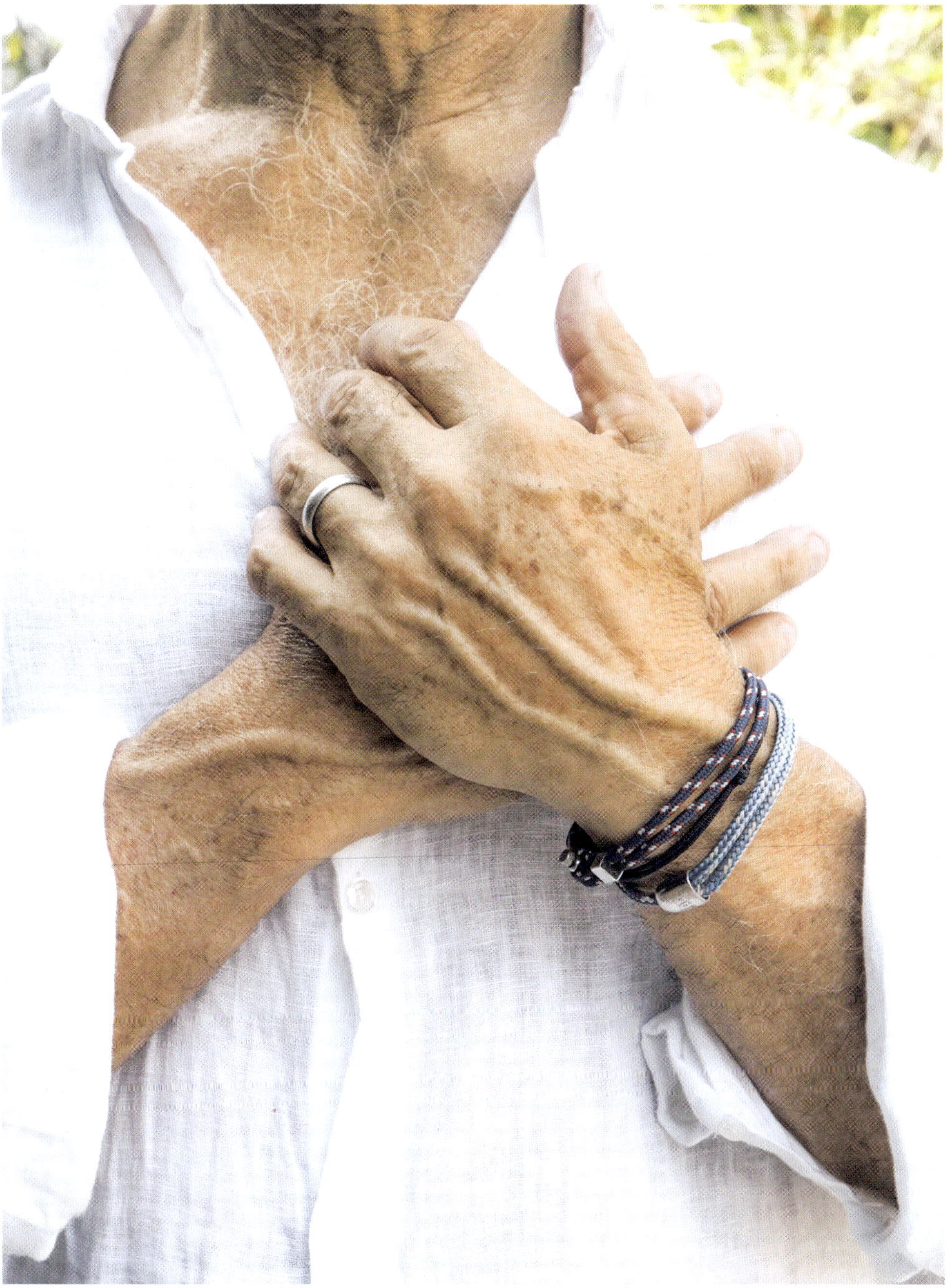

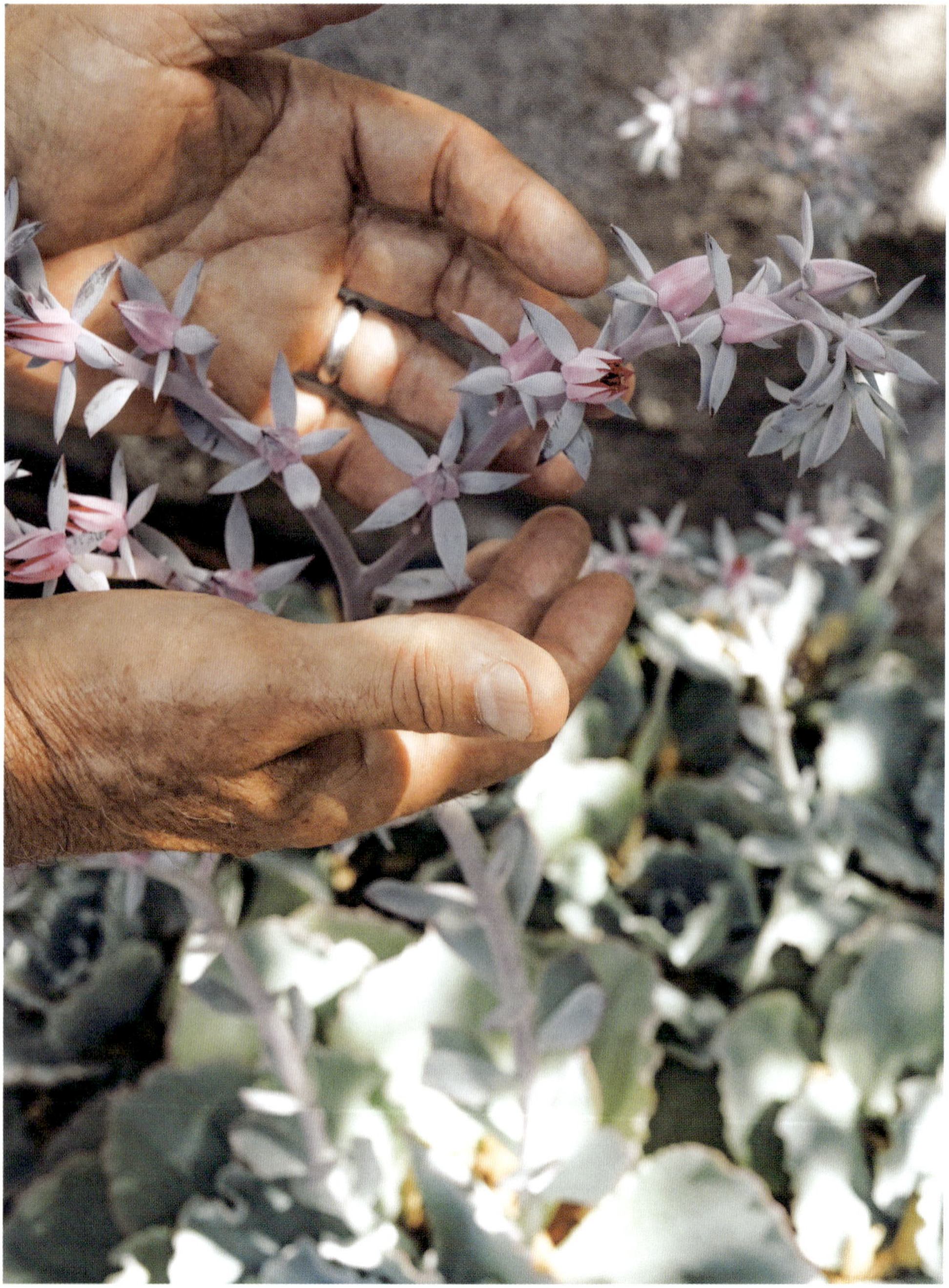

right now? How can I love myself?" When you have received wisdom, you can move on: "Heart, what do my loved ones need right now? What does my community need right now? What can I release?" Continue with any questions you seek answers to. The heart is very intelligent. If the mind wants to butt in and comment or interpret, gently remind it that it is time for the heart to speak.

» When you have received all the wisdom from your heart, you can write down anything that can be put into words, but don't *think* about it; just let it flow. You may write only words or phrases or even just sketch something. This is all okay; it doesn't have to make rational sense. As you practice this ceremony, you will get better at understanding what your heart has to say.

» This is a beautiful ceremony to practice regularly. The more you do it, the better you will become at turning off your mind and tuning in to your heart's wisdom.

PERSONAL GROWTH

Changing Mindset

INTENTION
Identify one limiting belief and transform it into a generative opportunity.

GROUP CEREMONY

TIME NEEDED
45 minutes

ELEMENTS
Paper and pen for each participant

Box of tissues

Candle or fire source

Burning bowl or vessel

The concept of "mindset" was popularized by Carol S. Dweck in her groundbreaking book *Mindset: The New Psychology of Success*. She identified two types of mindsets: growth mindset and fixed mindset. When you have a fixed mindset about something, you feel your qualities and life circumstances are set in stone, unable to be changed, leaving you needing to prove yourself over and over. When you have a growth mindset, you know that you are able to grow and change, allowing you to be open to learning rather than proving yourself.

Most of us carry a little bit of each of these mindsets in different parts of our lives. This ceremony will help you to identify a fixed mindset belief and transform it into a growth mindset opportunity. When you do this over and over, it can become a habit to view circumstances with a growth mindset. So, the advice is to perform this once and then again and again, at whatever interval works for you. It can be powerful to perform this ceremony with others so you can witness each other's growth and help each other break limiting beliefs that are holding you back.

STEPS

» Gather the group in a place where everyone has room to write and sit comfortably. Thank the group for investing in their mental health and being open to supporting each other.

» Start by reviewing fixed and growth mindsets with the group: People with a fixed mindset believe that they're born with specific intelligence, skills, and abilities that cannot

163

PERSONAL GROWTH

change; people with a growth mindset feel their skills and intelligence can be improved with effort and persistence.

» Have members of the group list some of their fixed mindset beliefs. Some examples are: "I am too old to switch careers," "My body is failing me," "I have to stay married," or "I cannot move out of the city I currently live in."

» Have each person write down at least three limiting beliefs about themselves on their own paper. This may bring up some emotion, so go slow here and have tissues on hand.

» Once complete, invite each person to choose one of their limiting beliefs about themselves and to transform it using a growth mindset. Encourage participants to write something down with a growth mindset lens, *even if they don't fully believe it*. The transformed statement should be in the present tense; for example, "I can't change careers" will transform to "I am changing careers" rather than "I can change careers." We can trick our mind by not just thinking about doing something but actually claiming it in the present tense.

» Finally, light a small fire or candle. One by one, have each person come to the center and read the limiting belief that they are transforming. Let them tear or crumple the paper, then add it to the fire or set it aflame. Then, have them state their reimagined belief. Have the group repeat their new belief back to them in acknowledgment.

» This is hard initially, but the more you practice it, the easier it gets. There are probably hundreds of beliefs you hold that feel fixed but are not. You can invite participants to pick a new fixed belief weekly, or even agree to meet together monthly to update each other on your progress or pick a new belief to transform.

PERSONAL GROWTH

Integration
TO CELEBRATE AN EXPERIENCE BEFORE MOVING ON

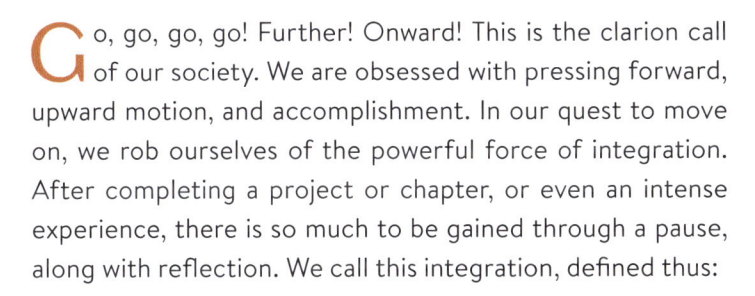

Go, go, go, go! Further! Onward! This is the clarion call of our society. We are obsessed with pressing forward, upward motion, and accomplishment. In our quest to move on, we rob ourselves of the powerful force of integration. After completing a project or chapter, or even an intense experience, there is so much to be gained through a pause, along with reflection. We call this integration, defined thus:

> *Integration is a process in which a person revisits and actively engages in making sense of, working through, translating, and processing the content of their ... experience. Through intentional effort and supportive practices, this process allows one to gradually capture and incorporate the emergent lessons and insights into their lives, thus moving toward greater balance and wholeness, both internally (mind, body, spirit) and externally (lifestyle, social relations, and the natural world).*
> —**GEOFF J. BATHJE, ERIC MAJESKI, MESPHINA KUDOWOR**
> "Psychedelic Integration: An Analysis of the Concept and Its Practice" (2022)

This ceremony invites you to gather wisdom and lessons from something you have experienced and begin integrating those lessons into your life before moving on to the next thing. Integration can take days or months, but if you do not thoughtfully focus on it, you will surely miss the rich lessons available to you from your experience.

You can do this alone or in a group. It doesn't have to be the group you had the experience with, but it can be helpful

INTENTION
Integrate the lessons of an experience you had into your life before moving on.

SOLO OR GROUP CEREMONY

TIME NEEDED
30 minutes

ELEMENTS
Candle

Objects that represent the project or experience

Pen and paper

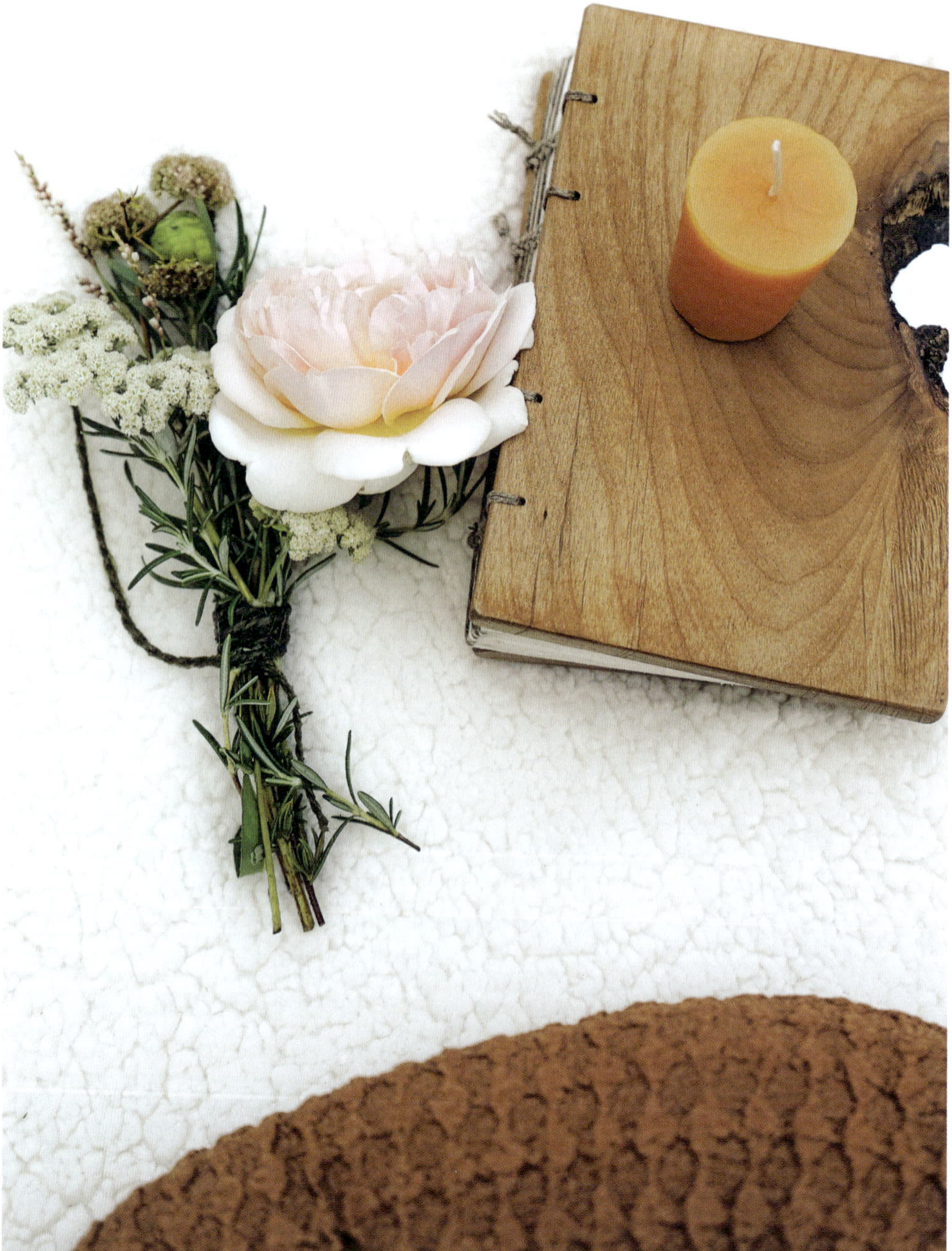

to have a common background. Enjoy this moment of rest and reflection before moving on.

STEPS

⇒ The best way to integrate an experience is to start with an intention before you start the experience, project, event, or trip. We often skip this important step, especially in work settings. The intention is different than the objective. An objective is what you want to accomplish, and an intention is a direction or area you want to explore, a guiding thought. See if you can get in the habit of setting an intention before you start something, and let your intention be with you as you move through the experience. You can write it down or just repeat it internally. An intention might be "To be open to the lessons this project will teach me," or "To act with grace and ease even when it becomes stressful."

⇒ While you are going through the experience or project, write down any insights or feelings that come to you. You don't have to analyze them fully at this time; you just have to capture them. If appropriate, capture anything that triggered the feeling. If you are working on a big project, you may want to have a dedicated journal for your thoughts.

⇒ When you have completed the project or experience, prepare to integrate and celebrate. Invite those involved in the project to join you or invite a trusted friend willing to listen as you reflect and process. Think about a location that will most reflect the completion of the project—it may be at home, a restaurant, a park, or a special destination.

⇒ Invite your group to gather in a circle, and light a candle in the middle with the objects that represent the experience or project.

(continues)

PERSONAL GROWTH

» Start by reviewing your intention for the project. If you did not write this down in advance, try to remember back to what you intended to get out of the project or what you intended to learn. Write this down at the top of a paper. Now write down everything that you felt or experienced during the project. What happened? What was good? What did not go well? What surprised you? What did you learn? Who showed up? How was the experience different from what you expected? Keep writing until you have captured it all. If you have notes from throughout the project, review those and see what has changed now that it has ended. If you are in a group, have each person do this.

» When you are done, review your notes and circle the parts that feel most important, or group the thoughts into categories. If you are in a group, invite each person to share their key insights. See if the insights are similar. Notice whether you all had the same experience or a different experience.

» When you are complete, gather around the candle and acknowledge the end of the project or experience together. You can hold hands, put your arms around each other, or just stand side by side. Thank the project or experience for everything that it taught you and provided to you. Let it know that you are grateful and will remember the lessons it brought. Blow out the candle together, signifying the end of the experience.

» Finally, celebrate together! Enjoy a meal, a treat, a libation. Toast each other and the experience you had together. Invite each person to take a pause before starting anything new—maybe just an hour, maybe a month, depending on the intensity and duration of what you are completing. Review the lessons from the experience frequently and continue to explore with curiosity what has changed in your life now.

PERSONAL GROWTH

Celebrating Friendship

Friends are some of the most cherished gifts of life. Yet how often do we actually celebrate our friendships? We celebrate birthdays and big events, but why not celebrate friendship itself and create deeper meaning and bonds through our actions? It can be wonderful to repeat this ceremony yearly, celebrating the friend (or friends) who make your life better by intentionally focusing on the gifts your friend brings to your life.

This ceremony is written for you to celebrate one of your friends, but you can easily adapt it for a group of friends celebrating friendship together by following the prompts at the end.

STEPS

» Find a quiet and somewhat protected space, such as your living room, backyard, or a local park under a tree.

» Lay the items from your friendship and the yellow flower on a table or on the ground; arrange them thoughtfully, along with some offerings from the land you are on (rocks, flowers, leaves). The idea is to create a beautiful altar weaving together Nature and your significant items representing this friendship.

» Light the candle and burn some blessing herbs or incense. Play soothing music. (See the playlist recommendations in the Resources section, page 184.)

» When you are ready to begin the ceremony, invite your friend to stand or sit facing you. Invite both of you to close

INTENTION
Honor friendship and the gifts it brings to your life.

CEREMONY FOR TWO PEOPLE

TIME NEEDED
1 hour

ELEMENTS
Items that represent what friendship means to you or has brought to your life, such as a poem, book, crystal, mug, or piece of jewelry

Yellow flower (Roses are a traditional symbol of friendship, but any flower will work)

Natural objects from the land where the ceremony is being held

Candle

Blessing herbs or incense, such as sage, copal, cedar, or lavender

Soothing music

PERSONAL GROWTH

their eyes, take a few deep breaths, and become present to the moment. Now open your eyes and gaze at each other, inviting the feeling of love you have for each other.

» State your intention. You can say, "I wish to honor our deep friendship and how it has enriched and supported my life." Once you have said your intention, you could invite your friend to also state an intention. Invite them to express what they wish to honor about your friendship.

» Invite the four directions (East, South, West, North) and any of your ancestors, guides, gods, or spirits to join you in your circle and ceremony. You can speak these invitations out loud or silently. Ask them to witness and bless your ceremony and your friendship.

» Breathe deeply to calm your body. Now relax your thinking mind and begin to become aware of your heart. Let your heart become a bright white light, and let that light spread over your entire body and out into the space you have created, washing over you and your dear friend.

» When you are calm and connected by heart, begin to say what your friendship has brought into your life. As you speak out loud about the gifts your friend has brought to your life, you can invite them to speak about the gifts you have brought to theirs. You can honor laughter, support, comfort, advice, acceptance, fun, a safe place to cry, unconditional love, understanding, honesty, and anything else you are feeling. Keep saying these things from the heart until you have exhausted them.

» Now you can say these words to your friend: "I honor our friendship and all the ways that it supports and provides for us." Say it once, and then invite your friend to join you in saying it again. Feel it resonate in your body.

PERSONAL GROWTH

» Close the ceremony by thanking the guides who joined you for witnessing your love for each other. Thank each other for showing up to honor each other and for all that you are for each other.

» After the ceremony, do something you love: go for a walk, have a cup of coffee or a glass of wine, or share a meal.

» Know that you have created a sacred relationship with your friend and honored it in ceremony. Feel the sacredness of this special connection when you are together and even when you are not. Feel your bond in your heart and know that it supports you always.

(continues)

PERSONAL GROWTH

For a Group of Friends

To adapt this ceremony for a group, invite your group of friends, letting them know your intention and inviting them to bring an item that symbolizes friendship for the shared altar or a small gift for each participant.

When you are ready, gather your friends in a circle in your prepared space and follow the steps above, speaking to the gifts that the group of friends brings to you.

You can then have each person in the group pair up with one other person. Invite each pair to gaze into each other's eyes for about 1 minute. Invite them to allow love to shine through their gaze onto their partner, showing unconditional acceptance.

When the minute is up, invite them to name one specific thing they are thankful to the friend for. They could say, "Thank you for your friendship; I honor you for the sound advice you always give me," or "Thank you for always including me in your plans." When this is complete, if you have a bigger group, switch pairs, repeating the exercise until each participant has had a chance to gaze with each other participant.

An addition or alternative to doing pairs is to create a tribute card for each participant. Lay out blank sheets of paper or cardstock, each one with a friend's name on it. It can be a beautiful piece of stationery, or even a piece of artwork with some blank space. Share the pages around the circle and have each person write one appreciation or attribute of the person whose name is on the paper. At the end, each friend will go home with a keepsake reminding them of how special they are and why their friends love them.

When you are finished with the activity, have the group return to a circle. Hold hands and gaze around the circle of love and friendship. You can close the circle by releasing any guides that have joined you. Celebrate together with a nice meal or activity that you love.

PERSONAL GROWTH

Honoring Land and Mother Earth

Not very long ago, many humans lived in divine relationship with Nature, knowing that we were part of her and she was part of us. We recognized that Mother Earth provided everything we needed—food, water, shelter, clothing, medicine—and we respected our reliance on her. Much of modern human society relates to Earth differently, as a resource to be conquered and extracted from, where our needs are above hers. Many believe that this disconnect from Nature is part of what is creating anxiety and discontent in our lives, not to mention destroying the Earth.

This ceremony honors and reweaves the personal relationship you can have with Nature and an area of land. When you show your gratitude and truly begin to be in a loving relationship with land, you will see how she responds to you and delights in your attention and devotion. Like any relationship, being in a relationship with land requires time, attention, and reciprocity. We receive many gifts from the land, and this ceremony allows you to give back with a grateful heart.

STEPS

⇨ Before the ceremony begins, remove your shoes and walk barefoot on the land. Walk in silence and slowly, without any devices to distract you. Be very attuned to the land as you walk, listening with your entire presence. Open all of your senses to really see and feel the land. What does she feel like? Smell like? Look like? What do you hear? Can you taste

INTENTION
Give thanks to Mother Earth and cultivate your relationship with the land.

SOLO OR GROUP CEREMONY

TIME NEEDED
1–2 hours

ELEMENTS
Readings or songs

Shovel

Blankets

Offerings for the land (see suggestions on page 177)

Candles

Blessing herbs or incense

Drum or rattle

PERSONAL GROWTH

her offerings? Do you sense any spirits present? Do any messages speak to you through the elements, the breeze? Depending on the size of the land you are on, this could take up to an hour. You can sing to the land or whisper to her as you walk. Introduce yourself and tell her how grateful you are to be in a relationship with her.

» As you walk, see if there is an area of the land that feels like it is calling for an offering or like an energy center. This is the spot where you will hold your ceremony.

» If you choose to perform this ceremony with a group, it will be important to create an invitation that explains what you will be doing and asks participants to consider what offering they will bring. You can also invite them to bring readings or songs to sing, altar items that honor the Earth, soil, or something that represents the land that they wish to honor.

» To prepare for ceremony, dig a hole in the ground. Before you do, tell the Earth that you would like to create an offering for her, and would like to dig a hole in which to put gifts of devotion. When you receive a feeling of acceptance, dig a hole that feels appropriate—not too big, not too small.

» When you are ready, gather alone or with your group around the hole you have dug with your offerings. Lay out blankets or textiles and place your special objects on the ground, creating an Earth altar. You can light candles and burn incense or blessing herbs. Open the ceremony by speaking your gratitude to the Earth and the ancestors of the land you are on. Sing songs or play a drum or rattle, honoring the land and allowing your energy to align into a unified, grounded frequency of connection.

(continues)

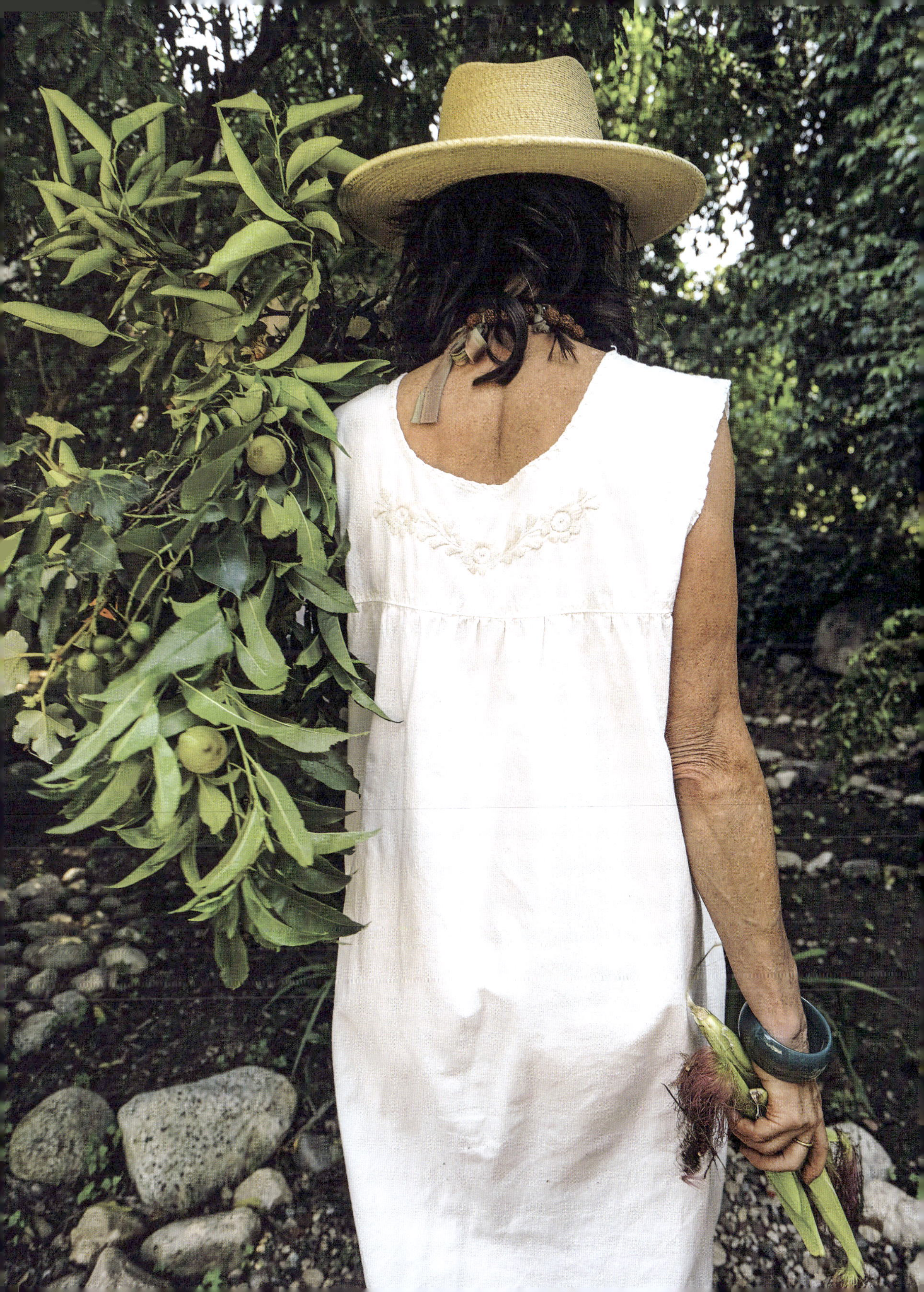

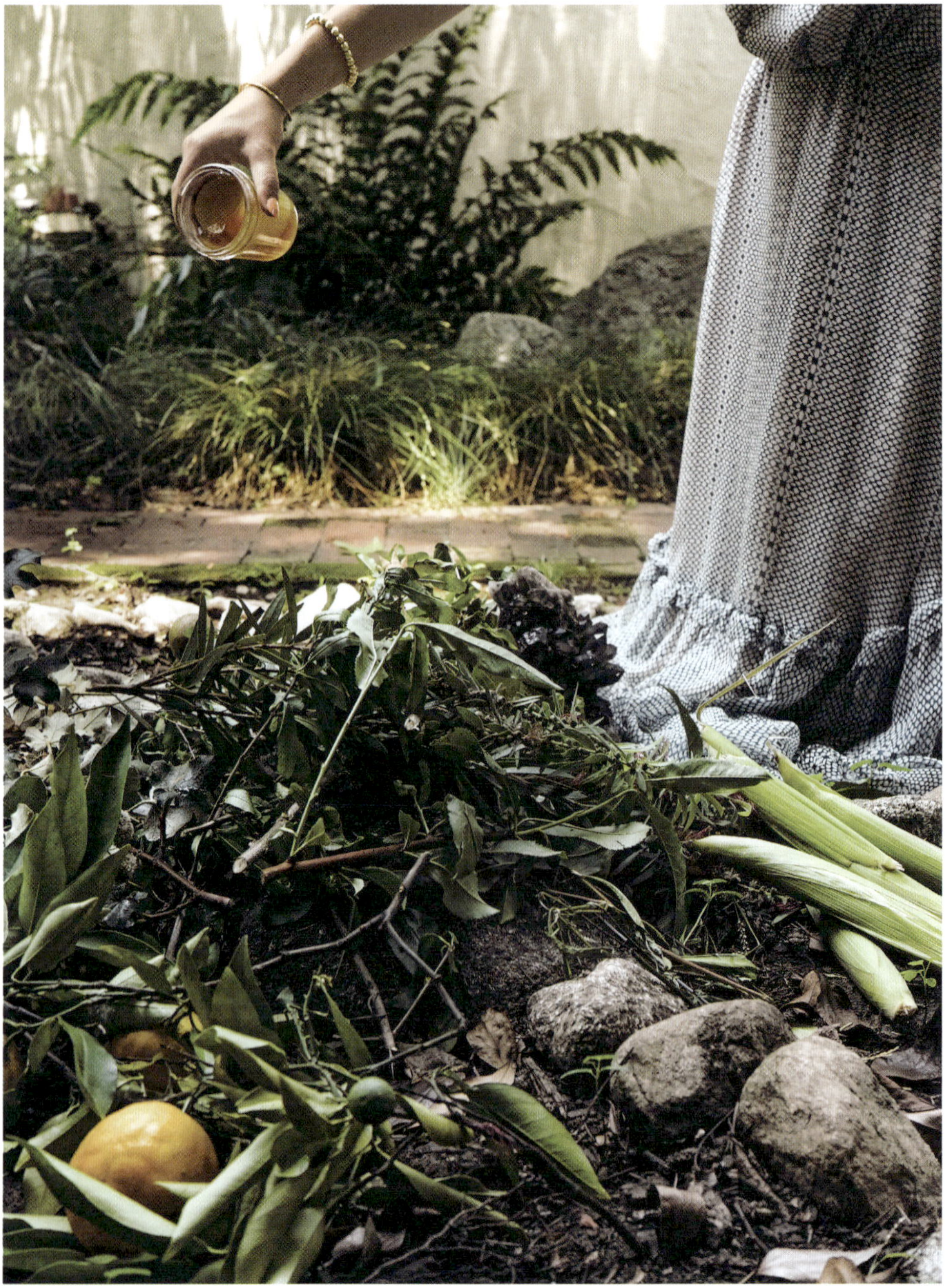

PERSONAL GROWTH

>> Approach the hole in the ground—one by one, if you are in a group—and offer the Earth your special offering. An offering should be something important to you, something that may be hard to part with, not something useless or leftover. As you consider your offering, listen to what the land is calling for or what you feel called to offer her in reciprocity for all she gives you. As you give your offering to the land, say clearly out loud what the offering is for. In a group setting, this can be whispered if it feels more private. You can say, "Thank you for the quiet respite you offer me when I want to calm down," or "Thank you, land, for providing a safe place for my children to play." You may also want to make your offering to benefit a place with suffering on the Earth, such as wildfires or floods. As each offering is made, others in the group will continue with singing or drumming to maintain the connection of group participation.

>> When the offerings have all been placed in the hole, you will cover them with earth, filling the hole and placing flowers on top. Breathe deeply with your hands on the Earth and send your wishes and prayers for the land out to all the places that need your devotion. Then close your circle with a prayer of gratitude.

>> Repeat often, by yourself or with others. This is a beautiful practice to honor your birthday, your ancestors, or special occasions centered around gratitude.

This ceremony was contributed by Rachel Jonta, a folk herbalist and land steward. She lives in relationship with an eighteen-acre farm in Oceanside, California, where she tends to the spirit of the land through offerings and ceremony.

Suggested Offerings for the Land

- Tears
- Songs and prayers
- Letters or a poem
- Sacred smoke or herbs
- Special foods
- Flowers
- Fruits and vegetables harvested from the land
- First sip of your cup of coffee
- Herbal medicines
- Milk or honey
- Water from a fresh spring or ocean
- Spirits or wine
- Tobacco
- Seeds
- Corn
- Crystals
- Carved wood or stone

Plan Your Own Ceremony

The following questions are intended to help you organize your own group ceremony. When imagining the ceremony, use a balance of your head and your heart—that is, don't plan too much on the logistics side, or too much on the ethereal side, but with a good balance of both. You want your ceremony to be connected to intuition and source but also to run smoothly. Good planning will ensure your ceremony has its best chance of succeeding for your intention and being something that you feel great about. You can find a printable version of this checklist online at shariboyer.com/ceremonyworksheet.

1. What is the intention of your ceremony? What is the desired outcome in the world?

   _____
   _____
   _____

2. Who will you invite? Include only those who are aligned with your purpose.

   _____
   _____
   _____
   _____
   _____

3. The invitation. Once you decide on the type (email, printed, etc.), be sure your invite includes:

   a. Your intention

   _____

   _____

   b. What to expect (length of time, what you will do, any special attire)

   _____

   _____

   c. What to bring (food, altar items, readings, music, instruments)

   _____

   _____

   d. Any prework you'd like them to do ("Think about X; write down Y")

   _____

   _____

   e. What to do if they have questions

   _____

   _____

   f. Location, date, time ("Please arrive on time and don't leave early")

   _____

   _____

4. Ceremony space preparation

   a. Define and mark the sacred space

   _____

   b. How participants will enter the sacred space

   _____
   _____

   c. Where the altar will go

   _____

   d. Items for the altar (earth, air, fire, water), items from Nature (flowers, rocks, branches), photographs, symbols

   _____
   _____

   e. Music or musical instruments

   _____
   _____

   f. Sacred smoke or incense

   _____

5. Roles for the ceremony *(The following roles are some examples. Your ceremony may require different roles than the ones listed here.)*

   a. Leader _____

   b. Fire keeper _____

   c. Water bearer_____

   d. Calling in the directions/guides/spirits

   _____

6. Flow of your ceremony
    a. Music, incense, sacred space setting
    b. Enter the sacred space
    c. Ground the group
    d. Invite ancestors, guides, and the four directions
    e. State your intention or purpose
    f. Perform the action or ritual that symbolizes the meaning or transformation you want to see
    g. Gather messages and notice any differences or transformations
    h. Sharing/journaling
    i. Open the circle; release the directions, spirits, or guides; restate the intention or ask what has happened and what is different in the world
    j. Exit the sacred space

7. Food or celebration
    a. How will you celebrate and relax together afterward?

    _____

    _____

    _____

8. Follow-up or integration
    a. Will you follow up with participants afterward to see how things are going or what transformations have taken place, and if so, on what cadence?

    _____

    _____

    _____

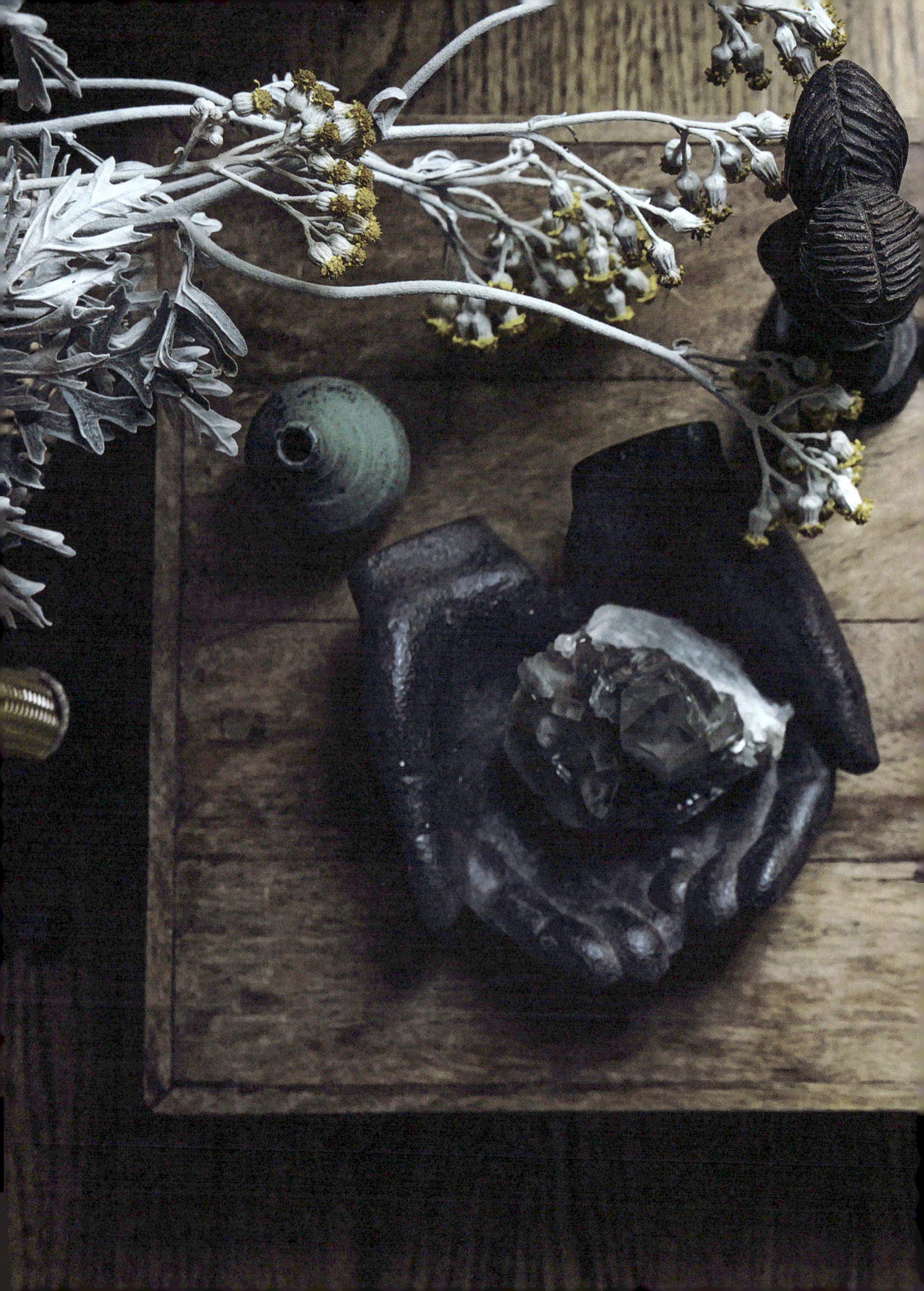

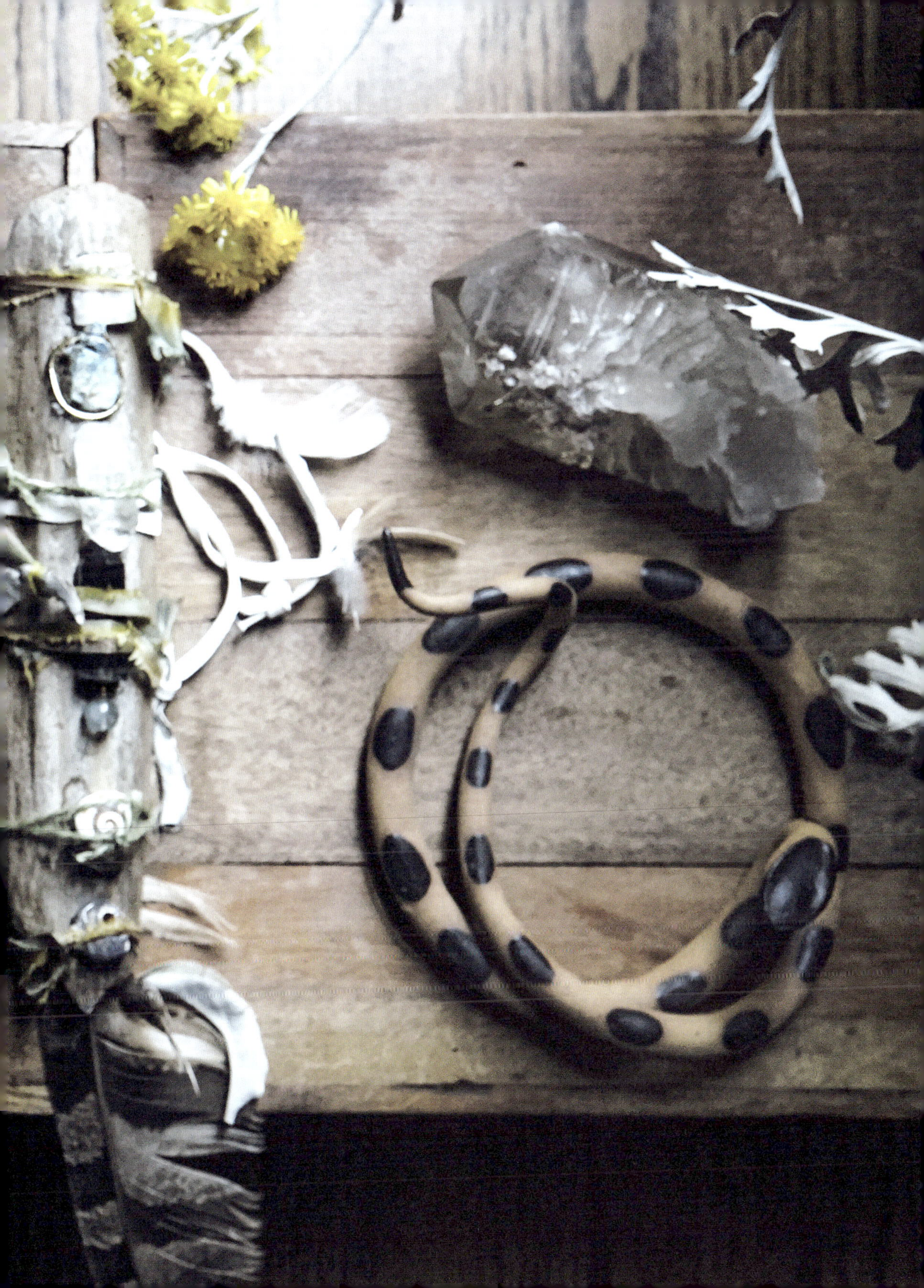

Resources

MUSIC FOR CEREMONY
- *The Book of Modern Ceremony* playlist: shariboyer.com/ceremonyplaylist
- Essie Jain, *To Love, As I Return*
- East Forest, *Music to Be Born To*, *Prana*
- Beautiful Chorus, *Hymns of Spirit*

CEREMONY PLANNING WORKSHEET
(shariboyer.com/ceremonyworksheet)

INCENSE AND BLESSING HERBS
- Oshala Farm—oshalafarm.com
  High-quality seasonal organic herbs, dried to order
- Mountain Rose Herbs—mountainroseherbs.com
  Great quality organic herbs in bulk
- Elemense Incense—elemensefragrance.com

ETSY.COM
- Great place to find handmade rattles, drums, candles, textiles, incense, chakapas, boxes, and handmade items for gifts

READINGS AND POEMS FOR CEREMONY
- Pixie Lighthorse: *Prayers of Honoring, Prayers of Honoring Voice, Prayers of Honoring Grief*
- Shahram Shiva: *Rumi: The Beloved Is You: My Favorite Collection of Deeply Passionate, Whimsical, Spiritual and Profound Poems and Quotes*
- Fiona Cook and Jessica Roux: *The Wheel of the Year: An Illustrated Guide to Nature's Rhythms*: Learn about the ancient holidays and customs that make up a year

RITUEL MALIBU (rituellife.com)
- Rituel creates custom retreats and ceremonies designed to connect you with self, spirit, and community.

SANCTUARY OF THE SACRED WILD (sanctuaryofthesacredwild.com)
- A nonprofit that teaches about living with the cycles of the seasons, gathering in ceremony, healing with plants, and earth tending.

MODERN ELDER ACADEMY (meawisdom.com)
- A modern-day wisdom school to help you navigate transitions, cultivate purpose, and unlock your potential. Online and in-person classes.

INSPIRATION
- *The Emerald Podcast:* A meditative podcast that explores myth, story, and imagination, and frequently references the role of ceremony and ritual in traditions around the world.
- *The Awakened Brain: The New Science of Spirituality and Our Quest for an Inspired Life* by Lisa Miller, PhD: Dr. Miller's discovery through neuroimaging that young people with a strong personal spiritual life are up 80 percent less likely to experience anxiety and depression was a major inspiration for writing *The Book of Modern Ceremony*.
- *The Art of Gathering: How We Meet and Why It Matters* by Priya Parker: Ms. Parker provides an exploration of how and why we gather, along with useful tips for enhancing your next gathering or ceremony.
- *Braiding Sweetgrass: Indigenous Wisdom, Scientific Knowledge, and the Teachings of Plants* by Robin Wall Kimmerer: A beautiful meditation on the natural world and our place in it. I highly recommend the audiobook read by the author.

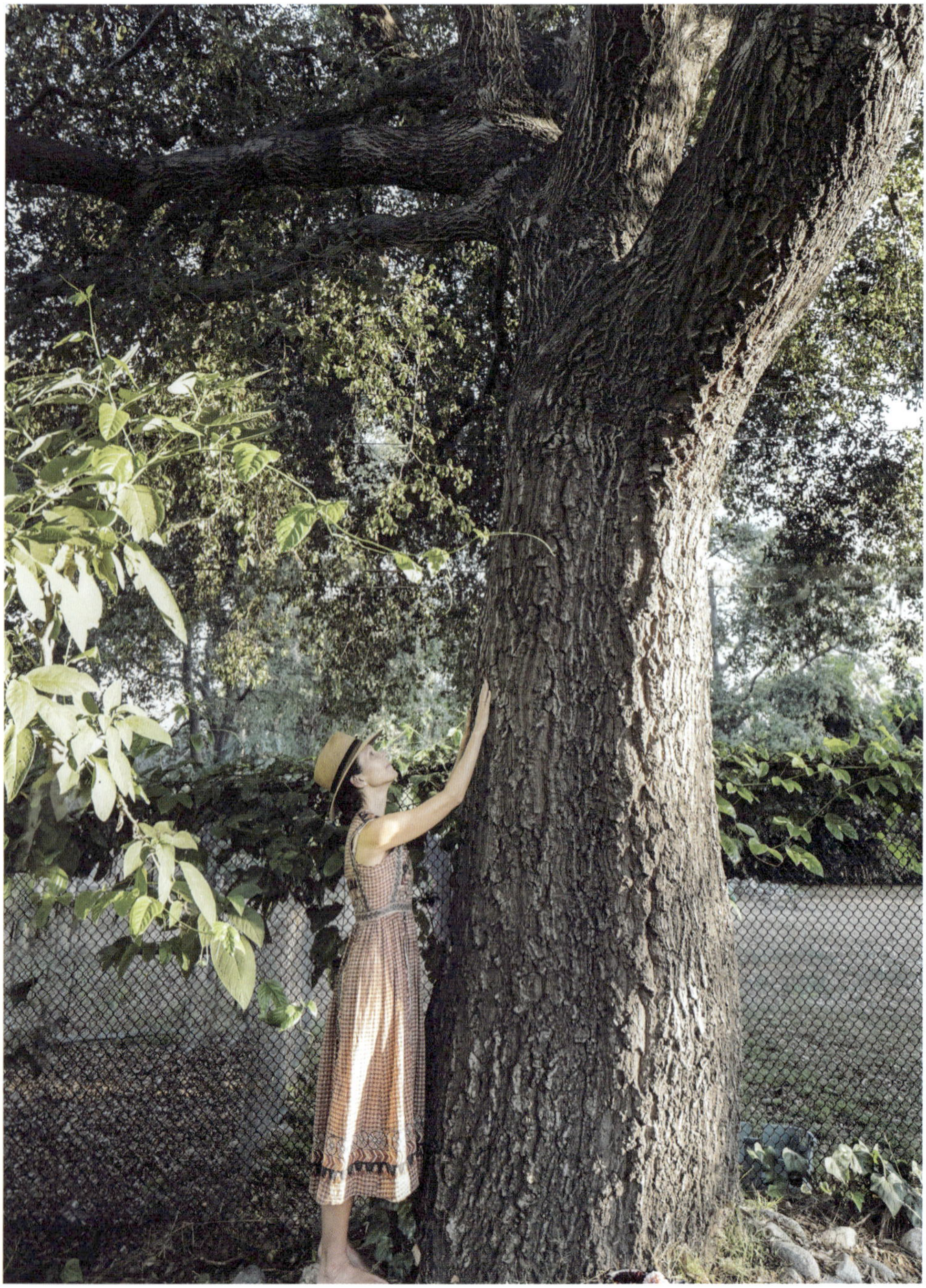

Acknowledgments

In 2020, amidst the fear and uncertainty of the COVID-19 pandemic, I enrolled in the School of the Sacred Wild. I had always wanted to learn about plant healing and herbalism, and I had, by coincidence, met the school's founder and instructor, Marysia Miernowska, at the Esalen Institute earlier in the year, just before the world shut down.

Marysia's teaching was a revelation for me. It completely changed me and my entire worldview. Learning about the world that Marysia inhabits was like finding Narnia at the back of the wardrobe: a magical world that existed fully intact, but unknown to me.

Each month, to introduce the plants and themes of the month, Marysia would hold an opening ceremony, and these quickly became my favorite part of this beautiful course. In ceremony, our coven (as we call ourselves) would gather, over Zoom, to join our hearts and minds together, and to step outside of time, in between worlds, where we could connect with the plants and learn about their gifts and healing properties. Marysia invited us to make ceremony days sacred by staying off technology and remaining quiet and meditative to prepare our bodies, minds, and spirits to receive the love and wisdom created during the ceremony. These ceremonies profoundly moved me.

I felt Alive.
Connected.
Fully present.
Loved.
Held.

The most astonishing thing was the feeling that all I was learning I was *remembering*, not learning anew. It was as if the knowledge Marysia was imparting already lived within me and was simply being reactivated.

Moved by my experiences, I began to research ceremony. I found surprisingly little written about it, outside of religious ceremony. An idea began to take hold of me for writing *The Book of Modern Ceremony* that would make ceremony accessible to our modern society. The only way to explain this is to say that the book *visited* upon me, exactly as described by author Elizabeth Gilbert in her book *Big Magic*. But I am not an author; I have no history of writing books or publishing anything. So why was this idea visiting *me*? *Haunting* me in the most positive sense, even while I worked full-time at a demanding job and cared for my family.

Finally, in late 2022, I left my job and decided to write the book, even if only for myself, just to get it down on paper. By then, I had gathered ideas, scientific facts, quotes, and inspiration for *The Book of Modern Ceremony* and sketched the outline of the book's contents. I had a vision of exactly what it would look like—set up like a recipe book to make the ceremonies easy to access and perform. Every time I sat down to write, the words flowed out of me as if coming from somewhere else.

Then something miraculous happened. I was at a retreat at the Modern Elder Academy in Baja, California (it's as amazing as it sounds—look it up!), where we were working to uncover our life's purpose. Of course, the book and performing ceremony kept coming up for me. As I was talking about the book idea one day, a woman next to me said that she had been in publishing her whole career and was a literary agent, and she was sure she could find a publisher for the book. *What the heck?* I thought. *If this book really wants to be in the world, then great, the doors will open.* And they did. My literary agent, Laura Yorke, connected me to my fantastic editor, Mary Ellen O'Neill at Workman Publishing, and *The Book of Modern Ceremony* was on its way into the world.

Next, I had to face my fears and insecurity about not being an author, not having any authority—basically, imposter syndrome—and write the book. What I discovered was that the process required deep trust and openness. My role was to be the curator, investigator, and channel for the ideas that wanted to be presented. The ideas that the world *needs* right now. I am humbled to have been the one chosen to deliver the message. But I did not do it alone.

Along the way, many teachers appeared. Mel Day reminded me that writing itself should be a ceremony. Rachel Jonte, Eve Gaines, Christy Billock, Marysia Miernowska, and her daughter Flora inspired me with their ceremonies. My close friends participated with me while I experimented with ceremonies for all occasions. Authors Lisa Miller (*The Awakened Brain: The New Science of Spirituality and Our Quest for an Inspired Life*) and Priya Parker (*The Art of Gathering: How We Meet and Why It Matters*) deeply inspired me, though I do not have the pleasure of knowing them. Chip Conley, founder of Modern Elder Academy and author of twelve books, also has a strong interest in rituals from around the world and kindly shared his research with me. Louesa Roebuck (*Punk Ikebana: Reimagining the Art of Floral Design*) inspired the visual layout and feel of the book. Alexandra Poer styled the photos using her visual brilliance, and Lauren Purves captured the images that evoke the emotions I wanted readers to feel. The Billocks allowed us to shoot at their beautiful and soulful home. Josh Schrei and his incredible podcast, *The Emerald*, provide inspiration continuously, often discussing the power of ritual and ceremony.

I want to express gratitude and love to my parents, Fern and Hank Dunbar, who instilled in me a deep love of nature early in my life by taking me to wild places every summer, and to all of my ancestors and guides. Finally, thank you to my husband, Chris, and sons, Tristan and Dylan, for encouraging me at every step of the way and acting as (mostly) willing participants in my ceremonies.

Shari Dunbar Boyer
Altadena, California
2024

Index

agreements, for circle ceremony, 38–39
altars
 location for, 27
 offerings for, 28
 planning and, 17
arches, 33
Autumnal Equinox, 50–51, 60–62

Bathje, Geoff J., 165
Beltane, 50–51
birthdays, untraditional, 109–110
bread, 33

candles, 33
celebrants, description of, 23
celebrating friendship, 169–172
celebration, as part of ceremony, 31
ceremony
 being in, 5–6
 common symbols for, 33
 description of, 4
 follow-up after, 31
 history of, 1
 holding, 27–31
 for life events, 77–147
 for personal growth, 149–177
 planning and holding, 11–33, 178–181
 preparing to perform, 24, 27
 purpose of, 6–9, 12, 15
 ritual versus, 5
 seasonal, 43–75
Ceremony Planning Worksheet, 11, 178–181
chalices, 33
changing mindset, 162–164
circle ceremony, 37–39
cleansing and renewal, 152–154
cleansing another person, 154
clearing stale energy, 121
closing the space, 29
Collings, Jane Hardwicke, 138
coming of age
 for boys, 100–105
 for girls, 94–99
commitment, 122–125
connection, loss of, 6
consciousness, other realms of, 4
cultural appropriation, 5
cups, 33

directions
 inviting, 28
 representations of four, 19
divorce, 126–129
doorways, 33
Durkheim, Émile, 6

elements
 planning and, 16–20
 representations of classical, 19

energy, clearing stale, 121
entrance, creating, 27, 28

family ceremonies
 remembering home, 106–108
 Samhain, 63–65
 See also group ceremonies
feathers, 33
fire, 33
follow-up, post-ceremony, 31
food, planning and, 20
friendship, celebrating, 169–172
funeral, living, 144–147

graduates, mothers of, 87–93
graduation, 83–86
group ceremonies
 blessing new home, 118–121
 celebrating friendship, 172
 celebrating motherhood, 80–82
 changing mindset, 162–164
 circle ceremony, 37–39
 coming of age, for boys, 100–105
 coming of age, for girls, 94–99
 commitment, 122–125

191

dealing with illness, 134–137
graduation, 83–86
honoring land and Mother Earth, 173–177
integration, 165–168
living funeral, 144–147
menopause, 138–143
mothers of graduates, 87–93
New Year, 73–75
retirement, 130–133
saying goodbye to house and land, 114–117
Summer Solstice, 56–59
Thanksgiving, 66–67
untraditional birthdays, 109–110
Vernal Equinox, 53–55
groups
  gathering, 28
  power of, 6, 8
  welcoming and harmonizing, 28
guest lists, developing, 15. *See also* invitations

harmonizing groups, 28
heart, connecting to wisdom of, 158–161
helping roles, description of, 23
herbs, planning and, 19
home/house
  blessing new, 118–121
  remembering, 106–108
  saying goodbye to, 114–117

illness, dealing with, 134–137
Imbolc, 50–51
incense, 19, 33
integration, 165–168
intention
  closing space and, 31
  ritual symbolizing, 29
  setting, 12, 15
  stating, 28
invitations, planning and, 20–21. *See also* guest lists

Kimmerer, Robin Wall, 30
Kudowor, Mesphina, 165

land
  honoring, 173–177
  saying goodbye to, 114–117
life events, ceremonies for
  about, 78
  blessing new home, 118–121
  celebrating motherhood, 80–82
  coming of age, for boys, 100–105
  coming of age, for girls, 94–99
  commitment, 122–125
  dealing with illness, 134–137
  divorce, 126–129
  graduation, 83–86
  living funeral, 144–147
  menopause, 138–143

mothers of graduates, 87–93
remembering home, 106–108
retirement, 130–133
saying goodbye to house and land, 114–117
untraditional birthdays, 109–110
listening from the heart, 39
living funeral, 144–147
location, determining, 16
Lughnasadh, 50–51

Majeski, Eric, 165
menopause, 138–143
mindset, changing, 162–164
moon ceremonies
  about, 46
  full moon, 49
  new moon, 48
Mother Earth, honoring, 173–177
motherhood, celebrating, 80–82
mothers of graduates, 87–93
music, planning and, 17

nature, objects from, 19
Nature-based festivals, 50–51
Nepo, Mark, 9
New Year, 73–75

organizer, description of, 23

pen and paper, planning and, 20

personal growth,
  ceremonies for
  about, 150
  celebrating friendship,
    169–172
  changing mindset,
    162–164
  cleansing and renewal,
    152–154
  connecting to wisdom
    of the heart, 158–161
  honoring land and
    Mother Earth,
    173–177
  integration, 165–168
  protection and
    strength, 155–157
poems, planning and, 20
protection and strength,
  155–157
purpose
  as filter, 15
  setting, 12, 15

readings, planning and,
  20
reciprocity, objects from
  nature and,
  19
renewal, cleansing and,
  152–154
resources, 184–185
retirement, 130–133
ritual
  ceremony versus, 5
  symbolizing intention,
    29
  roles, planning and, 23

Samhain, 50–51, 63–65
seasonal ceremonies
  about, 44
  Autumnal Equinox,
    60–62

moon ceremonies,
  46–49
New Year, 73–75
Samhain, 63–65
Summer Solstice,
  56–59
Thanksgiving, 66–67
Vernal Equinox, 53–55
Winter Solstice, 70–71
seating, circle formation
  for, 27
sharing, 29
soil, 33
solo ceremonies
  Autumnal Equinox,
    60–62
  cleansing and renewal,
    152–154
  connecting to wisdom
    of the heart, 158–161
  dealing with illness,
    134–137
  divorce, 126–129
  full moon, 49
  honoring land and
    Mother Earth,
    173–177
  integration, 165–168
  new moon, 48
  New Year, 73–75
  protection and
    strength, 155–157
  Samhain, 63–65
  Winter Solstice, 70–71
space
  closing, 29, 31
  setting up ceremonial,
    27
speaking from the heart,
  39
stale energy, clearing,
  121
strength, protection
  and, 155–157

string, 33
Summer Solstice, 50–51,
  56–59
symbols
  for classical elements,
    19
  common, 33
  role of, 4

talking pieces, 39
teas, planning and, 20
Thanksgiving, 66–67
tree branches, 33
two-person ceremonies
  celebrating friendship,
    169–172
  commitment, 122–125

Vernal Equinox, 50–51,
  53–55

water, 33
welcoming groups, 28
wheel of the year, 50–51
Winter Solstice, 50–51,
  70–71
wisdom
  connecting to, 158–161
  gathering, 29
  inner, 4
  receiving, 4

yarn, 33
year, wheel of, 50–51

SHARI DUNBAR BOYER is a ceremonialist and trained herbalist. She has been studying plant medicines, natural healing modalities, and the use of ceremony in modern and traditional cultures for over a decade. Shari came to ceremony after a long career in marketing, seeking ways to create more meaning and connection in her life and her community. She now creates and performs ceremonies for all types of events and transitions. Shari lives with her husband, Chris, two young adult sons, Tristan and Dylan, and two dogs on a property she is fortunate to tend at the foot of the San Gabriel mountains, with a suburban farm in Altadena, California. You can connect with Shari and learn more about her offerings at shariboyer.com or @sharidunbarboyer.